VOGUE® KNITTING

CROCHETED
BAGS

on the go!™

VOGUE® KNITTING

CROCHETED
BAGS

SIXTH&SPRING BOOKS
NEW YORK

SIXTH&SPRING BOOKS
233 Spring Street
New York, New York 10013

Library of Congress Cataloging-in-Publication Data

Library of Congress Control Number: 2005934943

ISBN: 1-931543-98-4
ISBN-13: 978-1-931543-98-9

Manufactured in China

1 3 5 7 9 10 8 6 4 2

First Edition, 2006

TABLE OF CONTENTS

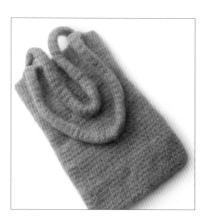

INTRODUCTION

Are you one of those people who appreciate the need to always pair that special outfit with the ideal handbag? Wouldn't that bag be even more perfect if it was a product of your own nimble fingers?

If so, then look no further. Perusing these pages, you will find dozens of thrilling, beautiful crochet designs at your fingertips.

Stunning photographs and easy-to-follow designs line each and every page, as some of today's foremost crochet designers share their proudest work with you. Whether you need a bag for a formal engagement or a picnic in the park, we are sure you will find the perfect piece.

There's nothing more beautiful and special than work from the heart—whether it's a design for yourself or a gift for a beloved friend or family member. These lovely handbags allow you to share a piece of yourself, and quite possibly become the most stylish woman on the block! So pick up your hook, pick out some yarn to match your latest favorite outfit, and get ready to **CROCHET ON THE GO!**

THE BASICS

Crochet is accessible and really quite easy to learn. Stitches are formed by pulling loops through other loops or stitches with a hook, creating a simple chain that is used in all patterns. Unlike knitting, there is no balancing act with stitches, shifting them from one needle to another; in crochet, one hand does all the work, and finished fabric lays away from the hook, letting crocheters concentrate on only the newest stitch they need to make. And, unlike other crafts, correcting a mistake is fairly stress-free—simply tug on the yarn to easily pull out the stitches you have worked.

If you're not convinced that it's easy to learn to crochet, perhaps the bags in this collection will inspire you. They run the gamut from the most basic stitches to more complicated ones, giving experienced crocheters ample selection and offering novices the chance to graduate to more difficult projects as they progress. The Casual Clutch on page 44 is a breeze to crochet and looks good with or without the embroidery. The Circular Stitch Tote on page 69 is simply a circle worked in single crochet stripes, then folded in half to form the bag, For more of a challenge, try the Cinched Stretch Bag on page 75. This design combines post stitches with a spiral pattern along with stripes just for fun.

And just as it is easy to learn crochet, it is also easy to finish. Though crocheted pieces often lack stretchability, again, depending on the yarn used, they usually lay flat without further blocking or finishing.

Handbags, purses, backpacks, totes or pouches—one thing is for sure, a woman never leaves home without one of them. Whether your bag holds your wallet and a few grooming necessities or acts as a small suitcase, the handbag you choose to carry is probably one of the most important accessories in your wardrobe.

On the following pages you'll find a variety of bags to fit every taste, season, age, and mood—not to mention skill level.

You'll find a wide assortment of shapes and sizes suitable for everything from a trip to the beach to a night on the town. Many of the larger totes can double as wonderful knitting bags—a unique way to carry around your on-the-go projects.

STRUCTURE OF BAGS
Crocheting a bag is a simple undertaking. Many of the designs in this collection are based on squares or rectangles—think of it as knitting a large-scale swatch with some finishing. Most have a single- or

double-fold flap with a loop and button or tassel-trimmed closure.

Other bags have side gussets to add width to the inside of the bag. In some cases the gussets may continue on to become straps; in others, separate straps are sewn on. There are also several designs with envelope-style flaps with a V- or U-shaped styling.

Several of the bags are finished with purchased ready-made plastic or wooden handles and are closed with a decorative button, buckle or brooch, such as the Evening Bag on page 82.

BAG FABRIC

Bags require a firm fabric. The dense nature of crochet fabric lends itself wonderfully to bags. This can be accomplished by working in a tighter gauge than average for the particular yarn. To achieve a tighter gauge, crochet with hooks that are two or three sizes smaller than is recommended on the ball band.

Another method is to felt the crocheted bag, such as the Felted Tote on page 30. The combination of hot water and agitation from the washing machine solidifies the fabric and gives added structure.

YARN SELECTION

For an exact reproduction of the bag photographed, use the yarn listed in the Materials section of the pattern. We've selected yarns that are readily available in the U.S. and Canada at the time of printing. The Resources list on page 92 provides addresses of yarn distributors. Contact them for the name of a retailer in your area.

YARN SUBSTITUTION

You may wish to substitute yarns. Perhaps you have a spectacular yarn you've been dying to try, maybe you view small-scale projects as a chance to incorporate leftovers from your yarn stash, or the yarn specified may not be available in your area. Bags allow you to be creative, but you'll need to crochet tothe given gauge to obtain the

CROCHET HOOKS					
14 steel	.60mm	C/2	2.50mm	I/9	5.50mm
12 steel	.75mm	D/3	3.00mm	J/10	6.00mm
10 steel	1.00mm	E/4	3.50mm		6.50mm
6 steel	1.50mm	F/5	4.00mm	K/10.5	7.00mm
5 steel	1.75mm	G/6	4.50mm		
B/1	2.00mm	H/8	5.00mm		

Categories of yarn, gauge ranges and recommended needle and hook sizes

Yarn Weight Symbol & Category Names	1 Super Fine	2 Fine	3 Light	4 Medium	5 Bulky	6 Super Bulky
Type of Yarns in Category	Sock, Fingering, Baby	Sport, Baby	DK, Light Worsted	Worsted, Afghan, Aran	Chunky, Craft, Rug	Bulky, Roving
Knit Gauge Range* in Stockinette Stitch to 4 Inches	27–32 sts	23–26 sts	21–24 sts	16–20 sts	12–15 sts	6–11 sts
Recommended Needle in Metric Size Range	2.25–3.25 mm	3.25–3.75 mm	3.75–4.5 mm	4.5–5.5 mm	5.5–8 mm	8 mm and larger
Recommended Needle U.S. Size Range	1 to 3	3 to 5	5 to 7	7 to 9	9 to 11	11 and larger
Crochet Gauge* Ranges in Single Crochet To 4 Inches	21–32 sts	16–20 sts	12–17 sts	11–14 sts	8–11 sts	5–9 sts
Recommended Hook in Metric Size Range	2.25–3.5 mm	3.5–4.5 mm	4.5–5.5 mm	5.5–6.5 mm	6.5–9 mm	9 mm and larger
Recommended Hook U.S. Size Range	B–1 to E–4	E–4 to 7	7 to I–9	I–9 to K–10½	K–10½ to M–13	M–13 and larger

*Guidelines only: The above reflects the most commonly used needle or hook sizes for specific yarn categories.

Beginner
Ideal first project.

Very Easy Very Vogue
Basic stitches, minimal shaping, simple finishing.

Intermediate
For crocheters with some experience. More intricate stitches, shaping and finishing.

Experienced
For crocheters able to work patterns with complicated shaping and finishing.

finished measurements with the substitute yarn. Make pattern adjustments where necessary. Be sure to consider how different yarn types (chenille, mohair, bouclé, etc.) will affect the final appearance of your bag.

Some of the most common fibers used for bags are acrylics or blends for washability, rayon or rayon blends for durability and strength. If you plan to felt your bag it is best to use 100 percent wool or wool blended with alpaca, mohair, or cashmere.

To facilitate yarn substitution, *Vogue Knitting* grades yarn by the standard stitch gauge obtained in stockinette stitch. You'll find a grading number in the Materials section of the pattern, immediately following the fiber type of the yarn. Look for a substitute yarn that falls into the same category. The suggested needle size and gauge on the ball band should be comparable to that on the Yarn Symbols chart on p.12.

After you've successfully gauge-swatched a substitute yarn, you'll need to figure out how much of the substitute yarn the project requires. First, find the total length of the original yarn in the pattern (multiply number of balls by yards/meters per ball). Divide this figure by the new yards/meters per ball (listed on the ball band). Round up to the next whole number. This is the number of balls required to knit your project.

READING CROCHET INSTRUCTIONS

If you are used to reading knitting instructions, then crochet instructions may seem a little tedious to follow. This is because crochet instructions use more abbreviations and punctuations and fewer words than traditional knitting instructions. Along with the separation of stitches and use of brackets, parentheses, commas, and other punctuation, there are numerous repetitions going on within a single row or round. Therefore, you must pay closer attention to reading instructions while you

EMBROIDERY STITCHES

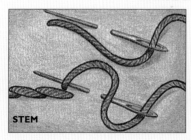
STEM

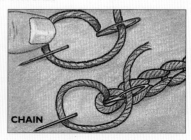
CHAIN

crochet. Here are a few explanations of the more common terminology used in this book.

Use of Parentheses ( )

Sometimes parentheses will be used to indicate the stitches that will be worked all into one stitch, such as "in next st work ( )" or "( ) in next st."

First st, Next st

The beginning stitch of every row is referred to as the "first st." When counting the turning chain (t-ch) as one stitch, the row or round will begin by starting to work into the next st (that is, skip the first st or space or whatever is designated in the pattern).

Stitch Counts

Sometimes the turning chain that is worked at the end (or beginning) of a row or a round will be referred to as 1 stitch and then is counted in the stitch count. When the t-ch is counted as 1 stitch, you will work into the next stitch, thus skipping the first stitch of the row or round. When the t-ch is not counted as a stitch, work into the first stitch.

Stitches Described

Sometimes the stitches are described as sc, dc, tr, ch-2 lp, 2-dc group, etc. and sometimes—such as in a mesh pattern of sc, ch 1—each sc and each ch-1 will be referred to as a st.

Back loop

Along the top of each crochet stitch or chain there are two loops. The loop farthest away from you is the "back loop."

Front Loop

Along the top of each crochet stitch or chain there are two loops. The loop closest to you is the "front loop."

Joining New Colors

When joining new colors in crochet, whether at the beginning of a row or while working across, always work the stitch in the old color to the last 2 loops, then draw the new color through the 2 loops and continue with the new color.

Working Over Ends

Crochet has a unique flat top along each row that is perfect for laying the old color across and working over the ends for several stitches. This will alleviate the cutting and weaving in of ends later.

Form a Ring

When a pattern is worked in the round, as in a square or medallion, the beginning chains are usually closed into a ring by working a slip stitch into the first chain.

TASSELS

Cut a piece of cardboard to the desired length of the tassel. Wrap yarn around the cardboard. Knot a piece of yarn tightly around one end, cut as shown, and remove the cardboard. Wrap and tie yarn around the tassel about 1"/2.5cm down from the top to secure the fringe.

Then on the first round, stitches are usually worked into the ring and less often into each chain.

BLOCKING

Blocking crochet is usually not necessary. However, in those cases when you do need to smooth out the fabric, choose a blocking method according to the yarn-care label and, when in doubt, test your gauge swatch. Note that some yarns, such as chenilles and ribbons, do not benefit from blocking.

Wet Block Method

Using rustproof pins, pin scarf to measurements on a flat surface and lightly dampen using a spray bottle. Allow to dry before removing pins.

Steam Block Method

Pin scarf to measurements with wrong side of the fabric facing up. Steam lightly, holding the iron 2"/5cm above the work. Do not press the iron onto the piece, as it will flatten the stitches.

ASSEMBLY

Most bags are made in one piece. Some are made circularly, therefore no seaming is required. Some are made in squares or rectangles, then folded in half with side seams. Some bags have a separate gusset that is sewn between the front and back pieces.

Seaming can be done using any of these methods:

1 Sewing, using the traditional whipstitch seaming method.

2 Crocheting, using either slip stitch or single crochet.

LINING

Adding a fabric lining to your bag has several advantages. It hides the sometimes unfinished look of the "wrong side" of the work, adds strength, and can create an interesting design element. The best fabrics to use are washable woven fabrics such as broadcloth, silk, or felt. Use the crocheted bag as a template to cut out the fabric, adding ½"/1.25cm seam allowance on all sides. Sew the pieces together as you did for the crocheted pieces. With wrong sides together, place the sewn fabric inside the crocheted band, turn down the top edge and slip stitch it in place.

CARE

Refer to the yarn label for the recommended cleaning method. Many of the bags in the book can be either washed by hand or in the machine on a gentle or wool cycle, in lukewarm water with a mild detergent. Do not agitate and don't soak for more than 10 minutes. Rinse gently with tepid water, then fold in a towel and gently press the water out. Lay flat to dry, away from excess heat and light. Check the yarn band for any specific care instructions such as dry-cleaning or tumble-drying.

CHAIN

I *Pass the yarn over the hook and catch it with the hook.*

2 *Draw the yarn through the loop on the hook.*

3 *Repeat steps 1 and 2 to make a chain.*

SINGLE CROCHET

I *Insert the hook through top two loops of a stitch. Pass the yarn over the hook and draw up a loop—two loops on hook.*

2 *Pass the yarn over the hook and draw through both loops on hook.*

3 *Continue in the same way, inserting the hook into each stitch.*

HALF-DOUBLE CROCHET

I *Pass the yarn over the hook. Insert the hook through the top two loops of a stitch.*

2 *Pass the yarn over the hook and draw up a loop—three loops on hook. Pass the yarn over the hook.*

3 *Draw through all three loops on hook.*

DOUBLE CROCHET

I *Pass the yarn over the hook. Insert the hook through the top two loops of a stitch.*

2 *Pass the yarn over the hook and draw up a loop— three loops on hook.*

SLIP STITCH

Insert the crochet hook into a stitch, catch the yarn and pull up a loop. Draw the loop through the loop on the hook.

3 *Pass the yarn over the hook and draw it through the first two loops on the hook, pass the yarn over the hook and draw through the remaining two loops. Continue in the same way, inserting the hook into each stitch.*

CROCHET TERMS AND ABBREVIATIONS

approx approximately

beg begin(ning)

CC contrast color

ch chain(s)

cm centimeter(s)

cont continue(ing)

dc double crochet (UK: tr-treble)

dec decrease(ing)–Reduce the stitches in a row (work stitches together or skip the stitches).

foll follow(s)(ing)

g gram(s)

hdc half double crochet (UK: htr-half treble)

inc increase(ing)—Add stitches in a row (work extra stitches into a stitch or between the stitches).

LH left-hand

lp(s) loop(s)

m meter(s)

MC main color

mm millimeter(s)

oz ounce(s)

pat(s) pattern

pm place markers—Place or attach a loop of contrast yarn or purchased stitch marker as indicated.

rem remain(s)(ing)

rep repeat

rnd(s) round(s)

RH right-hand

RS right side(s)

sc single crochet (UK: dc-double crochet)

sk skip

sl st slip stitch (UK: single crochet)

sp(s) space(s)

st(s) stitch(es)

t-ch turning chain

tog together

tr treble (UK: tr tr-triple treble)

WS wrong side(s)

work even Continue in pattern without increasing or decreasing (UK: work straight).

yd yard(s)

yo yarn over—Wrap the yarn around the hook (UK: yrh).

* = repeat directions following * as many times as indicated.

[ ] = Repeat directions inside brackets as many times as indicated.

FLOWER BAG
Garden party

Designed by Helen Eaton, this flower-patterned bag is ideal for the funky bohemian in all of us.

▥ Approx 9"/23cm wide x 12"/30.5cm high (excluding handles)

MATERIALS

▥ 2 1¾ oz/50g balls (each approx 125yds/113m) of Plymouth Yarn Company *Baby Alpaca DK* (alpaca) in #3317 seafoam (MC) (3)

▥ 1 ball in #4148 medium blue (CC)

▥ Size E/4 (3.5mm) crochet hook *or size to obtain gauge*

▥ ¼yd/.25m of lining fabric

▥ Matching thread

GAUGES

25 sts and 11 rows to 4"/10cm over mesh st using size E/4 (3.5mm) hook.

Small flower to 2"/5cm using size E/4 (3.5mm) hook.

Medium flower to 2½"/6.5cm using size E/4 (3.5mm) hook.

Large flower to 3"/7.5cm using size E/4 (3.5mm) hook.

Take time to check gauges.

Note

Bag is made in one piece.

BAG

With MC, ch 126.

Row 1 Sc in 10th ch from hook, *ch 5, skip next 3 ch, sc in next ch; rep from * across. Ch 6, turn.

Row 2 *Sc in next ch-5 sp, ch 5; rep from *, end sc in last ch-5 sp, ch 2, dc in 4th ch of ch-9 of row 1. Ch 6, turn.

Row 3 Sc in first ch-5 sp, *ch 5, sc in next ch-5 sp; rep from * across. Ch 6, turn.

Row 4 *Sc in next ch-5 sp, ch 5; rep from *, end sc in last ch-5 sp, ch 2, dc in 4th ch of ch-6 of row below. Ch 6, turn. Rep rows 3 and 4 for mesh st and work even until piece measures 11½"/29cm from beg, end on row 4. Ch 5, turn.

TOP EDGING

Next row Sc in first ch-5 sp, *ch 3, sc into next ch-5 sp; rep from *, end ch 2, dc in last sc. Ch 1, turn.

Next row Sc in each st across. Ch 1, turn. Rep last row twice more. Fasten off.

HANDLE

With MC, ch 121.

Row 1 Sc in 2nd ch from hook and in each ch across—120 sts. Ch 1, turn.

Row 2 Sc in each st across. Ch 1, turn. Row 2 once more. Fasten off.

SMALL FLOWER

(make 5)

With CC, ch 6. Join ch with a sl st, forming a ring.

Rnd 1 Ch 1, work 12 sc in ring, join rnd with a sl st in first st.

Rnd 2 Ch 1, sc in first st, *ch 8, sc in next st; rep from * around, end ch 8, join rnd with a sl st in first st. Fasten off.

MEDIUM FLOWER
(make 2)
Work as for small flower to rnd 2.
Rnd 2 Ch 1, sc in first st, *ch 12, sc in next st; rep from * around, end ch 12, join rnd with a sl st in first st. Fasten off.

LARGE FLOWER
(make 4)
Work as for small flower to rnd 2.
Rnd 2 Ch 1, sc in first st, *ch 18, sc in next st; rep from * around, end ch 18, join rnd with a sl st in first st. Fasten off.

FINISHING
Sew side edges of bag together. Center seam on back, then sew bottom edges together. Sew on flowers as pictured or as desired. On WS of each side edge, sew an end of handle to row 1 of top edging.

LINING
Measure, mark, and cut out two pieces of lining ½"/1.3cm larger all around than bag. With RS facing, and using a ½"/1.3cm seam allowance, sew pieces together along side and bottom edges. Turn top edge ½"/1.3cm to WS and press. Insert lining. Slipstitch top edge of lining in place.

SCALLOP SHELL BAG
Ruby Tuesday

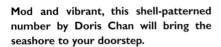

Mod and vibrant, this shell-patterned number by Doris Chan will bring the seashore to your doorstep.

FINISHED MEASUREMENTS
▨ Approx 14"/35.5cm wide x 9"/23cm high x 4"/10cm deep (excluding handles)

MATERIALS
▨ 5 1¾oz/50g balls (each approx 136yds/125m) of Patons *Grace* (cotton) in #60409 ruby ③
▨ Size F/5 (3.75mm) crochet hook *or size to obtain gauge*
▨ One pair of 7½"/19cm wide x 5"/12.5cm high D-shaped bamboo handles

GAUGE
4 spike shell rep to 5"/12.5cm and 4 rows to 4"/10 over pat st using size F/5 (3.75mm) hook.
Take time to check gauge.

STITCH GLOSSARY
Spike shell Yo, insert hook under ch-1 sp (between 2 shells) and into 3rd dc of shell of 2 rows below, yo, draw up a lp that's the same height as row you are working on, [yo, draw through 2 lps on hook] twice. Working in the same manner, work 4 more dc in same dc to complete spike shell.

BACK
Beg at top edge, ch 22.
Row 1 Sc in 2nd ch from hook and in each ch across—21 sts. Ch 3, turn.
Row 2 Dc in each st across. Ch 3, turn.

Row 3 Rep row 2. Ch 1, turn.
Row 4 Sc in each st across. Turn.

BEG SHELL PAT
Row 1 (RS) Ch 3 (counts as 1 dc), work 2 dc in first st (beg half-shell made), ch 1, [sk next 3 sts, work 5 dc in next st, ch 1] 4 times, sk next 3 sts, work 3 dc in last st (half-shell made)—4 whole shells and 2 half-shells. Turn.
Row 2 Ch 1, sc in first st, ch 1, [work spike shell over next ch-1 sp and 2nd sc of row below, ch 1] 5 times, end sc in 3rd ch of beg ch-3 of row below—5 spike shells.
Row 3 Ch 3 (counts as 1 dc), work 2 dc in first st (beg half-shell made), ch 1, [work spike shell over next ch-1 sp and 3rd dc of shell of 2 rows below, ch 1] 4 times, work 3 dc in last st—4 spike shells and 2 half-shells. Turn.
Row 4 Ch 3 (counts as 1 dc), work 2 dc in first st (beg half-shell made), ch 1, [work spike shell over next ch-1 sp and 3rd dc of shell of 2 rows below, ch 1] 5 times, work 3 dc in in 3rd ch of beg ch-3 of row below—5 spike shells and 2 half-shells. Turn.
Row 5 Ch 1, sc in first st, ch 1, work spike shell over next ch-1 sp and 2nd dc of 2 rows below, ch 1, [work spike shell over next ch-1 sp and 3rd dc of 2 rows below, ch 1] 4 times, end work spike shell over next ch-1 sp and 2nd dc of 2 rows below, ch 1, sc in 3rd ch of beg ch-3 of row below—6 spike shells.
Row 6 Ch 1, sc in first st, ch 1, work spike

shell over next ch-1 sp and 2nd dc of 2 rows below, ch 1, [work spike shell over next ch-1 sp and 3rd dc of 2 rows below, ch 1] 5 times, end work spike shell over next ch-1 sp and 2nd dc of 2 rows below, ch 1, sc in 3rd ch of beg ch-3 of row below—7 spike shells.

Row 7 Ch 3 (counts as 1 dc), work 2 dc in first st (beg half-shell made), ch 1, [work spike shell over next ch-1 sp and 3rd dc of shell of 2 rows below, ch 1] 6 times, work 3 dc in in 3rd ch of beg ch-3 of row below—6 spike shells and 2 half-shells. Turn.

Row 8 Ch 3 (counts as 1 dc), work 2 dc in first st (beg half-shell made), ch 1, [work spike shell over next ch-1 sp and 3rd dc of shell of 2 rows below, ch 1] 7 times, work 3 dc in in 3rd ch of beg ch-3 of row below—7 spike shells and 2 half-shells. Turn.

Row 9 Ch 1, sc in first st, ch 1, work spike shell over next ch-1 sp and 2nd dc of 2 rows below, ch 1, [work spike shell over next ch-1 sp and 3rd dc of 2 rows below, ch 1] 6 times, end work spike shell over next ch-1 sp and 2nd dc of 2 rows below, ch 1, sc in 3rd ch of beg ch-3 of row below—8 spike shells.

Row 10 Ch 3 (counts as 1 dc), work 2 dc in first st (beg half-shell made), ch 1, [work spike shell over next ch-1 sp and 3rd dc of shell of 2 rows below, ch 1] 7 times, work 3 dc in in 3rd ch of beg ch-3 of row below—7 spike shells and 2 half-shells.

Turn.

Row 11 Ch 3 (counts as 1 dc), work 2 dc in first st (beg half-shell made), ch 1, [work spike shell over next ch-1 sp and 3rd dc of shell of 2 rows below, ch 1] 8 times, work 3 dc in in 3rd ch of beg ch-3 of row below—8 spike shells and 2 half-shells. Turn.

Row 12 Ch 1, sc in first st, ch 1, work spike shell over next ch-1 sp and 2nd dc of 2 rows below, ch 1, [work spike shell over next ch-1 sp and 3rd dc of 2 rows below, ch 1] 7 times, end work spike shell over next ch-1 sp and 2nd dc of 2 rows below, ch 1, sc in 3rd ch of beg ch-3 of row below—9 spike shells.

Row 13 Ch 3 (counts as 1 dc), work 2 dc in first st (beg half-shell made), ch 1, [work spike shell over next ch-1 sp and 3rd dc of shell of 2 rows below, ch 1] 8 times, work 3 dc in in 3rd ch of beg ch-3 of row below—8 spike shells and 2 half-shells. Turn.

Row 14 Ch 3 (counts as 1 dc), work 2 dc in first st (beg half-shell made), ch 1, [work spike shell over next ch-1 sp and 3rd dc of shell of 2 rows below, ch 1] 9 times, work 3 dc in in 3rd ch of beg ch-3 of row below—9 spike shells and 2 half-shells. Turn.

Row 15 Ch 1, sc in first st, ch 1, work spike shell over next ch-1 sp and 2nd dc of 2 rows below, ch 1, [work spike shell over next ch-1 sp and 3rd dc of 2 rows below, ch 1] 8 times, end work spike shell over next ch-1 sp and 2nd dc of 2 rows below, ch 1, sc in 3rd ch of beg ch-3 of row below—10 spike shells.

Row 16 Ch 3 (counts as 1 dc), work 2 dc in first st (beg half-shell made), ch 1, [work spike shell over next ch-1 sp and 3rd dc of shell of 2 rows below, ch 1] 9 times, work 3 dc in in 3rd ch of beg ch-3 of row below—9 spike shells and 2 half-shells. Turn.

Row 17 Ch 1, sc in first st, ch 1, [work spike shell over next ch-1 sp and 3rd dc of 2 rows below, ch 1] 10 times, end sc in 3rd ch of beg ch-3 of row below—10 spike shells.

Rows 18-32 Rep rows 16 and 17 for 7 times more, then row 16 once.

Row 33 Ch 1, sc in first st, [work spike shell over next ch-1 sp and 3rd dc of 2 rows below, sc in 3rd dc of next shell of row below] 10 times, end sc in 3rd ch of beg ch-3 of row below. Fasten off.

FRONT

Work as for back.

SIDE GUSSET

(make 2)
Ch 8.

Row 1 (WS) Work 2 dc in 4th ch from hook, ch 1, sk next 3 ch, work 3 dc in last ch—2 half-shells. Turn.

Row 2 Ch 1, sc in first st, ch 1, work spike shell over next ch-1 sp and 2nd sc of row below, ch 1, sc in 3rd ch of beg ch-3 of row

below—1 spike shell. Turn.

Row 3 Ch 3, work 2 dc in first st, ch 1, skip shell, work 3 dc in last st. Turn.

Row 4 Ch 3, work 2 dc in first st, ch 1, work spike shell over next ch-1 sp and 3rd dc of shell of 2 rows below, ch 1, work 3 dc in 3rd ch of beg ch-3 of row below—1 spike shell and 2 half-shells. Turn.

Row 5 Ch 1, sc in first st, ch 1, work spike shell over next ch-1 sp and 2nd dc of 2 rows below, ch 1, work spike shell over next ch-1 sp and 2nd dc of 2 rows below, ch 1, sc in 3rd ch of beg ch-3 of row below—2 spike shells.

Row 6 Ch 3, work 2 dc in first st, ch 1, work spike shell over next ch-1 sp and 3rd dc of shell of 2 rows below, ch 1, work 3 dc in 3rd ch of beg ch-3 of row below—1 spike shell and 2 half-shells. Turn.

Row 7 Ch 1, sc in first st, ch 1, [work spike shell over next ch-1 sp and 3rd dc of 2 rows below, ch 1] twice, sc in 3rd ch of beg ch-3 of row below—2 spike shells.

Row 8 Rep row 6.

Row 9 Ch 3, work 2 dc in first st, ch 1, [work spike shell over next ch-1 sp and 3rd dc of shell of 2 rows below, ch 1] twice, work 3 dc in in 3rd ch of beg ch-3 of row below–2 spike shells and 2 half-shells. Turn.

Row 10 Ch 1, sc in first st, ch 1, work spike shell over next ch-1 sp and 2nd dc of 2 rows below, ch 1, work spike shell over next ch-1 sp and 3rd dc of shell of 2 rows below, ch

1, work spike shell over next ch-1 sp and 2nd dc of 2 rows below, ch 1, sc in 3rd ch of beg ch-3 of row below—3 spike shells.

Row 11 Ch 3, work 2 dc in first st, ch 1, [work spike shell over next ch-1 sp and 3rd dc of shell of 2 rows below, ch 1] twice, work 3 dc in last st—2 spike shells and 2 half-shells. Turn.

Row 12 Ch 1, sc in first st, ch 1, [work spike shell over next ch-1 sp and 3rd dc of shell of 2 rows below, ch 1] 3 times, ch 1, sc in 3rd ch of beg ch-3 of row below—3 spike shells.

Rows 13-21 Rep rows 11 and 12 for 4 times more, then row 11 once.

Row 22 Ch 1, sc in first st, [work spike shell over next ch-1 sp and 3rd dc of 2 rows below, sc in 3rd dc of next shell of row below] twice, work spike shell over next ch-1 sp and 3rd dc of 2 rows below, sc in 3rd ch of beg ch-3 of row below. Turn.

Row 23 Sl st in each st across. Fasten off.

FINISHING
Lightly block pieces flat. Sew bottom edges of front and back together. To sc each side gusset to front and back, position and pin pieces together so WS are facing. With RS facing, join yarn with a sl st in top left corner of back.

Row 1 Ch 1, making sure that work lies flat, sc evenly along entire edge to top right corner of front. Fasten off. Rep for opposite gusset. To attach each handle, fold top edge of bag over handle to WS encasing handle; sew in place.

GRANNY SQUARE BAG
Purse pride

■■■▭

Gayle Bunn designed this beautiful tribute to the red, white, and blue— a patriotic bag perfect for July 4th or any day.

FINISHED MEASUREMENTS

▨ Approx 12½"/31.5cm wide x 17"/43cm high (excluding handle)

MATERIALS

▨ 3 1¾oz/50g balls (each approx 99yds/91m) of Needful Yarns/Filtes King *Extra* (wool) in #1100 dark blue (A) **4**
▨ 2 balls each in #2113 cream (B), #1863 light blue (C), and #2007 hot pink (D)
▨ Size H/8 (5mm) crochet hook *or size to obtain gauge*
▨ One 7½"/19cm wide x 6"/15cm high bamboo handle with gold handle clips
▨ One 12"/30.5cm matching zipper
▨ ½yd/.5m of lining fabric
▨ Matching thread

GAUGE

One square to 4¼"/10.5cm using size H/8 (5mm) hook.
Take time to check gauge.

Note

All rnds are worked on the RS.

STITCH GLOSSARY

dc2tog [Yo, insert hook into next st and draw up a lp, yo and draw through 2 lps on hook] twice, yo and draw through all 3 lps on hook.

dc3tog [Yo, insert hook into next st and draw up a lp, yo and draw through 2 lps on hook] 3 times, yo and draw through all 4 lps on hook.

BASIC GRANNY SQUARE

With first color, ch 4. Join ch with a sl st, forming a ring.

Rnd I (RS) Ch 3 (counts as 1 dc), work 2 dc in ring, [ch 3, work 3 dc in ring] 3 times, ch 3, join rnd with a sl st in 3rd ch of beg ch-3. Fasten off.

Rnd 2 Join 2nd color with a sl st in any corner ch-3 sp, ch 3 (counts as 1 dc), work (2 dc, ch 3, 3 dc) in same ch-3 sp, *ch 1, work (3 dc, ch 3, 3 dc) in next corner ch-3 sp; rep from * twice more, ch 1, join rnd with a sl st in 3rd ch of beg ch-3. Fasten off.

Rnd 3 Join 3rd color with a sl st in any corner ch-3 sp, ch 3 (counts as 1 dc), work (2 dc, ch 3, 3 dc) in same ch-3 sp, *ch 1, work 3 dc in next ch-1 sp, ch 1, work (3 dc, ch 3, 3 dc) in next corner ch-3 sp; rep from * twice more, ch 1, work 3 dc in last ch-1 sp, join rnd with a sl st in 3rd ch of beg ch-3. Fasten off.

Rnd 4 Join 4th color with a sl st in any corner ch-3 sp, ch 3 (counts as 1 dc), work (2 dc, ch 3, 3 dc) in same ch-3 sp, *[ch 1, work 3 dc in next ch-1 sp] twice, ch 1, work (3 dc, ch 3, 3 dc) in next corner ch-3 sp; rep from * twice more, [ch 1, work 3 dc in last ch-1 sp] twice, join rnd with a sl st in 3rd ch of beg ch-3. Fasten off. Make 14 squares (7 for front and 7 for back) foll placement diagram for colorways.

With B, ch 4. Join ch with a sl st, forming a ring.

Rnd 1 (RS) Rep rnd 1 as for basic square.

Rnd 2 With D, rep rnd 2 as for basic square.

Rnd 3 Join C with a sl st in any corner ch-3 sp, ch 3 (counts as 1 dc), work (2 dc, ch 3, 3 dc) in same ch-3 sp, ch 1, work 3 dc in next ch-1 sp, ch 1, *work (3 dc, ch 3, 3 dc) in next corner ch-3 sp, ch 1, work 3 dc in next ch-1 sp*, ch 3, work 3 sc in next ch-3 sp, ch 3, work 3 dc in next ch-1 sp, ch 1, rep from * to * once more, ch 1, join with sl st in 3rd ch of beg ch-3. Fasten off.

Rnd 4 Join A with a sl st in corner ch-3 sp opposite corner where 3 sc were worked, ch 3 (counts as 1 dc), work (2 dc, ch 3, 3 dc) in same ch-3 sp, [ch 1, work 3 dc in next ch-1 sp] twice, ch 1, work (3 dc, ch 3, 3 dc) in next corner ch-3 sp, ch 1, work 3 dc in next ch-1 sp, ch 1, work 3 sc in next ch-3 sp, sc in next sc, work 3 sc in next sc, sc in next sc, work 3 sc in next ch-3 sp, ch 1, work 3 dc in next ch-1 sp, ch 1, work (3 dc, ch 3, 3 dc) in next corner ch-3 sp, [ch 1, work 3 dc in next ch-1 sp] twice, ch 1, join rnd with a sl st in 3rd ch of beg ch-3. Fasten off.

RIGHT TOP CORNER HALF-SQUARE
(make 2)

With A, ch 4. Join ch with a sl st, forming a ring.

Rnd 1 (RS) Rep rnd 1 as for basic square.

Rnd 2 Join C with a sl st in any corner ch-3 sp, ch 3 (counts as 1 dc), work (2 dc, ch 3, 3 dc) in same ch-3 sp, ch 3, sc in next ch-3 sp, ch 3, [work (3 dc, ch 3, 3 dc) in next corner ch-3 sp, ch 1] twice (placing a yarn marker in first ch-3 sp worked), join rnd with a sl st in 3rd ch of beg ch-3. Fasten off.

Row 3 Join D with a sl st in marked corner ch-3 sp, ch 3 (counts as 1 dc), work 3 dc in same ch-3 sp, ch 1, work 3 dc in next ch-1 sp, ch 1, work (3 dc, ch 3, 3 dc) in next corner ch-3 sp, ch 1, work 3 dc in next ch-1 sp, ch 1, work 4 dc in next corner ch-3 sp. Fasten off, leaving rem sts unworked.

Row 4 Join B with a sl st in 3rd ch of beg ch-3 of row 3, ch 3 (counts as 1 dc), work 3 dc in same sp, [ch 1, work 3 dc in next ch-1 sp] twice, ch 1, work (3 dc, ch 3, 3 dc) in next corner ch-3 sp, [ch 1, work 3 dc in next ch-1 sp] twice, ch 3, sc in top of last dc of row 3, ch 3, work 2 dc in side edge of same dc of row 3, dc in ch-3 corner sp of rnd 2, dc in next 3 dc of rnd 2, dc in next ch-3 sp. Ch 3, turn.

Row 5 [Dc2tog] 3 times, dc in top of ch 3 of row 4—4 sts. Ch 3, turn.

Row 6 Dc3tog, dc in top of ch 3. Fasten off.

LEFT TOP CORNER HALF-SQUARE
(make 2)

Work as for right top corner half-square until row 3 is completed.

Row 4 (RS) Join B with a sl st in top of beg ch-3 of row 3, ch 3, dc in next 3 dc of rnd 2, dc in ch-3 corner sp of rnd 2, work 2 dc in side edge of dc of row 3, ch 3, sc in top of first dc of row 3, ch 3, [work 3 dc in next ch-1 sp, ch 1] twice, work (3 dc, ch 3, 3 dc) in next corner ch-3 sp, [ch 1, work 3 dc in net ch-1 sp] twice, ch 1, work 4 dc in last dc. Fasten off.

Row 5 With RS facing, join B with a sl st in 3rd ch of beg ch-3 of row 4, ch 3, [dc2tog] 3 times—4 sts. Ch 3, turn.

Row 6 Dc3tog, dc in top of ch 3. Fasten off.

FINISHING

Using A, sc squares tog foll placement diagram, joining squares across first to form strips, then join strips together to form front (or back) of bag.

Lining

Fold lining fabric in half, RS facing. Trace front onto lining fabric. Cut out pieces ½"/1.3cm larger all around. Using a ½"/1.3cm seam allowance, sew side and bottom seams. Trim seams to ¼"/.5cm. Make ½"/1.3cm deep clips along curved edges of top. Turn top edge ½"/1.3cm to WS and press. Set aside.

Edging

With RS facing, join A with a sl st in top right corner of bag back. **Row I** Ch 1, making sure that work lies flat, sc evenly along entire edge. Fasten off. Rep for bag front. To sc front and back tog, place pieces tog, WS facing. Working through both thicknesses, join A with a sl st in left top corner. **Row 2** Ch 1, making sure that work lies flat, sc evenly across side and bottom edges, working 3 sc in each bottom corner. Fasten off. Sew in zipper. Insert lining. Sew top edges of lining in place, having pressed edge approx ⅛"/.3cm from zipper teeth. Using A, whipstitch handle clips to each top corner.

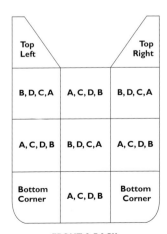

FRONT & BACK

29

Green with envy

■■■▨▢

Your friends will be positively green with envy when they see this adorable felted tote. Designed by Marty Miller.

▨ Approx 9"/23cm wide x 15"/38cm high (excluding handles)

MATERIALS
▨ 3 3½oz/100g skeins (each approx110yd/92m) of Reynolds/JCA Yarns *Lopi* (wool) each in #9965 chartreuse green heather (A) and #9964 golden heather (B) (**5**)
▨ Size N/15 (10mm) crochet hook *or size to obtain gauge*

GAUGE
8 sts to 4"/10cm over sc using size N/15 (10mm) hook before felting.
Take time to check gauge.

Notes
1 When changing colors, draw new color through when joining rnd with a sl st.
2 Do not carry up colors when working bag; cut and join them as needed.
3 When working handles, carry up colors loosely on WS.

BAG
With A, ch 26.
Rnd 1 Sc in 2nd ch from hook and in each ch across. Turn to bottom lps of foundation ch. Sc in first lp and in each lp across, join rnd with a sl st in first sc—50 sts.
Rnd 2 Ch 1, sc in each st around, join rnd with a sl st in first sc. Rep rnd 2 for pat st

and work stripe sequence as foll: work 8 rnds A, 1 rnd B, 5 rnds A, 1 rnd B, 3 rnds A, 2 rnds B, 2 rnds A, 3 rnds B, 1 rnd A, 5 rnds B, 1 rnd A, and 8 rnds B. Fasten off.

HANDLE
(make 2)
With A, ch 7, leaving a long tail.
Foundation row (RS) Sc in 2nd ch from hook and in each ch across—6 sts. Taking care not to twist foundation row, join row with a sl st in first sc.
Rnd 1 Ch 1, sc in each st around, join rnd with a sl st in first sc. Rep rnd 1 for pat st, working stripe sequence same as for bag. Fasten off, leaving a long tail.

FINISHING
Flatten bag and handles. Count 5 sts in from each side edge on front and back and mark with pins. Pin ends of handles to top edge of bag so outer edges are at pin marks. With RS together, and working through all three thicknesses, sc end of each handle to top edge of bag.

FELTING
Place bag in a zippered pillowcase cover. Fill washing machine to low water setting at a hot temperature. Add ¼ cup of a gentle detergent and the bag. Use 15 to 20 minute wash cycle, including cold rinse and spin. Check measurements of bag. Repeat process with progressively shorter cycles until measurements are achieved. Air-dry or machine-dry on a low setting. Steam block to finished measurements.

FUR-STRIPED PURSE
Jackie O

This hot fur-striped bag by Anna Mishka is like a time machine back to the magical days of Camelot.

FINISHED MEASUREMENTS
▨ Approx 14"/35.5cm wide x 12"/30.5cm high (excluding handles)

MATERIALS
▨ 2 3oz/85g balls (each approx 125yds/118m) of Lion Brand Yarn *Color Waves* (acrylic/polyester) in #341 mai tai (A) (**4**)
▨ 2 1¾oz/50g balls (each approx 60yd/54m) of Lion Brand Yarn *Fun Fur* (polyester) in #153 black (B) (**4**)
▨ Size I/9 (5.5mm) crochet hook *or size to obtain gauge*
▨ Four 32mm black plastic rings
▨ Stitch holders

GAUGE
14 sts and 14 rows to 4"/10cm over pat st using size I/9 (5.5mm) hook.
Take time to check gauge.

Notes
1 Bag is worked in the round with WS facing. After bag is completed, it is turned RS out.
2 When changing colors, draw new color through 2 lps on hook to complete last sc.

BAG
With A, ch 100. Taking care not to twist ch, join ch with a sl st in first ch, forming a ring.
Rnd 1 Ch 1, sc in same ch as joining, *ch 1, skip next ch, sc in next ch; rep from * around to last ch, end ch 1, skip last ch, join rnd with a sl st in first sc—100 sts.
Rnd 2 Sl st to first ch-1 sp, ch 1, sc in same sp as sl st, *ch 1, sc in next ch-1 sp; rep from * around, end ch 1, join rnd with a sl st in first sc, changing to B. Rep rnd 2 for pat st and work in stripe pat as foll: *1 rnd B and 2 rnds A; rep from * until bag measures 12"/20.5cm from beg, end with 1 rnd B. Fasten off

HANDLE
(make 2)
With 2 strands of A held tog, ch 62.
Row 1 (RS) Hdc in 3rd ch from hook and in each ch across—60 sts. Ch 3, turn.
Row 2 Skip first st, dc in each st across—59 sts. Fasten off.

FINISHING
Sew bottom seam. Turn bag RS out. Thread two rings onto each handle. Position end of each handle so outside edge is 3"/7.5cm from side edge of bag and bottom edge is 3"/7.5cm from top edge of bag. Sew bottom edge of each handle in place. Slide each ring down to base of handle, then sew across width, just above ring to secure in place. Fold each handle in half, WS facing, then whipstitch edges tog, beg and ending at height of top of bag.

Sunday best

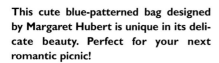

This cute blue-patterned bag designed by Margaret Hubert is unique in its delicate beauty. Perfect for your next romantic picnic!

FINISHED MEASUREMENTS
▓ Approx 11"/28cm wide x 14"/35.5cm high (not including strap)

MATERIALS
▓ 4 1¾oz/50g balls (each approx 121yds/111m) of Lana Grossa *Toccata Print* (cotton) in #339 blues (MC) **3**
▓ 1 1¾oz/50g ball (approx 121yds/111m) of Lana Grossa *Toccata* (cotton) in #204 dark blue (CC) **3**
▓ Size G/6 (4mm) crochet hook *or size to obtain gauge*
▓ ¼yd/.25m of lining fabric
▓ Matching thread

GAUGE
15 sts and 13 rows to 4"/10cm over cluster st using size G/6 (4mm) hook.
Take time to check gauge.

STITCH GLOSSARY
CL (cluster st) Yo, insert hook into ch (or st), yo, draw up a lp, yo and draw through 2 lps on hook, insert hook into next ch (or st), yo, draw up a lp, yo, draw through all 3 lps on hook.

BACK
With MC, ch 44.
Row I Work first CL over 4th and 5th ch from hook, *work next CL over last ch worked and next ch; rep from * to last ch, dc in last ch. Ch 3, turn.
Row 2 Work first CL over first 2 sts, *work next CL over last st worked and next st; rep from * across, end dc in top of ch-3 t-ch. Ch 3, turn. Rep row 2 for CL st and work even until piece measures 14"/35.5cm from beg. Fasten off.

FRONT
Work as for back.

FLOWER
With CC, ch 34.
Rnd I Work 2 dc in 4th ch from hook, then work 2 dc in each ch across. Ch 4, turn to bottom lps of foundation ch. Work 2 tr in each bottom lp across, join rnd with a sl st in first dc.
Rnd 2 Ch 1, sc in next st, *ch 4, sc in next st; rep from * around, join rnd with a sl st in first sc. Fasten off.

LEAF
(make 2)
With CC, ch 15.
Rnd I Dc in 4th ch from hook, dc in next 8 ch, hdc in next ch, sc in next ch, sl st in last ch 3, turn to bottom lps of foundation ch, sl st in first lp, sc in next lp, hdc in next lp, dc next 9 lps, ch 2, join rnd with a sl st in first dc.
Rnd 2 Ch 1, sc in each st to ch-3 sp, work 3 sc in ch-3 sp, sc in each st to ch-2 sp, work 2 sc in ch-2 sp, join rnd with a sl st in first sc. Fasten off.

FINISHING

To sc front and back tog, place pieces tog, WS facing. Working through both thicknesses, join CC with a sl st in top left corner.

Row 1 Ch 1, making sure that work lies flat, sc evenly across side and bottom edges, working 3 sc in each corner. Do not turn.

Row 2 Ch 1, working from left to right, sc in each st across three sides. Fasten-off.

TOP EDGING

With RS facing, join CC with a sl st in any side seam.

Rnd 1 Ch 1, sc in each st around, working 1 sc in each seam, join rnd with a sl st in first sc.

Rnd 2 Ch 1, working from left to right, sc in each st around, join rnd with a sl st in first st. Fasten-off.

TWISTED CORD STRAP

Cut a 12"/30.5cm strand of CC; set aside. Cut five 4yd/3.5m, long strands of CC. Put strands tog and fold in half. Tie ends into a knot. Holding the knot in your hand, slip the lp over a hook and pull tight. Slip a pencil through the knotted end, then rotate the pencil, twisting the cord until it starts to double back on itself. Put one finger in center of cord and carefully fold in half, letting two ends of cord twist together. Using 12"/30.5cm strand, tie securely about 1"/2.5cm from end. Draw each end of cord through to inside of bag 8"/20.5cm from bottom edge. Sew each end securely in place.

LINING

Cut two 11"/28cm x 9"/23cm pieces of lining. With RS facing, and using a ¼"/.6cm seam allowance, sew pieces tog along side and bottom edges. Turn top edge ½"/1.3cm to WS and press. Insert lining. Slipstitch top edge of lining in place. Fold flower in half so dc side is on top of tr side. Roll into flower shape, tacking rounds to secure. Sew flower to center of front flap, so edge of flower extends ½"/1.3cm beyond edge of bag. Sew on leaves, as shown.

FLORAL CLUTCH
Bountiful blossoms

This lovely beige beauty designed by Margaret Hubert caters to your craving for all that is frilly and feminine.

■ Approx 10½"/26.5cm wide x 5½"/14cm high

MATERIALS
■ 2 2.6oz/74g skeins (each approx 200yds/183m) of Lorna's Laces *Shepard Sport* (wool) in #15ns chino ⬤
■ Size E/4 (3.5mm) crochet hook *or size to obtain gauge*
■ ¼yd/.25m of lining fabric
■ ¼yd/.25m of heavy-weight interfacing
■ Matching thread
■ One 1½"/38mm button

GAUGE
19 sts and 11 rows to 4"/10cm over sc using size E/4 (3.5mm) hook.
One flower to 1½"/4cm using size E/4 (3.5mm) hook.
Take time to check gauges.

STITCH GLOSSARY
sc2tog [Insert hook into next st and draw up a lp] twice, yo and draw through all 3 lps on hook.

BACK
Ch 51.
Row 1 (WS) Sc in 2nd ch from hook and in each ch across—50 sts. Ch 1, turn.

Rows 2 and 3 Sc in each st across. Ch 1, turn.
Row 4 Sc2tog, sc in each st across to last 2 sts, sc2tog—48 sts. Ch 1, turn.
Rows 5-7 Rep row 2.
Rows 8-31 Rep rows 2-7 four times more, then row 2 once—40 sts. Ch 1, turn

FRONT FLAP
Row 32 (RS) Working through back lps only, sc in each st across. Ch 1, turn.
Rows 33-45 Sc in each st across. Ch 1, turn.
Row 46 Sc2tog, sc in each st across to last 2 sts, sc2tog—38 sts. Ch 1, turn.
Row 47 Sc in each st across. Ch 1, turn.
Rows 48-51 Rep rows 46 and 47 twice more—34 sts.
Row 52 Sc2tog, sc in next 14 sts, ch 5 for button lp, skip next 2 sts, sc in next 14 sts, sc2tog—32 sts. Fasten-off.

FRONT
Work as for back to row 31. Fasten-off.

GUSSET
Ch 7.
Row 1 Sc in 2nd ch from hook and in each ch across—6 sts. Ch 1, turn.
Row 2 Sc in each st across. Ch 1, turn. Rep row 2 for pat st and work even until piece measures same length as sides and bottom edge of front. Fasten-off.

FLOWER

(make 38)

Ch 4.

Join ch with a sl st, forming a ring.

Rnd 1 Ch 1, work 10 sc in ring, join rnd with a sl st in first sc.

Rnd 2 *Ch 2, work 3 dc in next st, sl st in next st; rep from * around 4 times more. Fasten off.

FINISHING

Trace bag front twice onto interfacing; set aside. With RS of front facing, sc gusset to side and bottom edges. Fasten off. With RS of back facing, sc gusset to side and bottom edges. Fasten-off.

LINING

Cut out interfacing ¼"/.5cm smaller all around. Test fit into bag; trim if necessary. Trace one interfacing piece twice onto lining fabric. Cut out ½"/1.3cm larger all around. On WS of each lining piece, position an interfacing piece in center. Fold edges of lining over to WS and press. Turn bag WS out. Slipstitch linings to front and back; turn RS out. Sew flowers onto flap. Sew on button.

You'll have endless possibilities for filling these adorable crocheted baskets, designed by Carol Ventura.

Small basket
▪ Approx 4"/10cm diameter x 4½"/11.5cm high
Medium basket
▪ Approx 7¾"/19.5cm diameter x 7"/17.5cm high
Large basket
▪ Approx 9"/19.5cm diameter x 10¼"/26cm high

MATERIALS
Small basket
▪ 2 skeins (each approx 60yds/55m) of Caron International *Aunt Lydia's Craft and Rug Yarn* (polyester) in #0420 brown (MC) ⬛
▪ 1 skein in #0905 natural (CC)
Medium basket
▪ 4 skeins in #0905 natural (MC)
▪ 1 skein in #0405 beige (CC)
Large basket
▪ 8 skeins in #0405 beige (MC)
▪ 3 skeins in #0420 brown (CC)
▪ Size 00 (3.5mm) steel crochet hook or size to obtain gauge
▪ Safety pin

GAUGE
24 sts and 20 rnds to 4"/10cm over tapestry sc using size 00 (3.5mm) steel hook.
Take time to check gauge.

Notes
1 To work tapestry sc, work over the color not in use on every rnd.
2 When changing colors, draw new color through 2 lps on hook to complete a sc.

SMALL BASKET
With MC, ch 4, leaving a 6"/15cm long tail. Join ch with a sl st, forming a ring.
Rnd 1 Work 6 sc in ring, working over tail. Mark last st made with the safety pin. You will be working in a spiral, marking the last st made with the safety pin to indicate end of rnd.
Rnd 2 Cont to work over the tail, work 2 sc in each st around—12 sts. Cut the tail flush with sts, then beg to work over CC as foll:
Rnd 3 Work 2 sc in each st around—24 sts.
Rnd 4 * Sc in next st, work 2 sc in next st; rep from * around—36 sts.
Rnd 5 Sc in each st around.
Rnd 6 * Sc in next 2 sts, work 2 sc in next st; rep from * around—48 sts.
Rnd 7 * Sc in next 3 sts, work 2 sc in next st; rep from * around—60 sts.
Rnd 8 * Sc in next 4 sts, work 2 sc in next st; rep from * around—72 sts.
Rnd 9 Sc in each st around.

BEG CHART
Next rnd Work 18-st rep of rnd 1 of chart 4 times. Cont to foll chart in this way to rnd 17.

Next 2 rnds Sc in each st around, changing to CC in last st of last rnd.

Last 2 rnds With CC and working over MC, sc in each st around. Sl st in next st, fasten off.

MEDIUM BASKET

Work as for small basket until rnd 9 is completed.

Rnd 10 * Sc in next 5 sts, work 2 sc in next st; rep from * around—84 sts.

Rnd 11 * Sc in next 6 sts, work 2 sc in next st; rep from * around—96 sts.

Rnd 12 * Sc in next 7 sts, work 2 sc in next st; rep from * around—108 sts.

Rnd 13 Sc in each st around.

Rnd 14 * Sc in next 8 sts, work 2 sc in next st; rep from * around—120 sts.

Rnd 15 * Sc in next 9 sts, work 2 sc in next st; rep from * around—132 sts.

Rnd 16 * Sc in next 10 sts, work 2 sc in next st; rep from * around—144 sts.

Rnd 17 Sc in each st around.

Beg chart

Next rnd Work 18-st rep of rnd 1 of chart 8 times. Cont to foll chart in this way to rnd 17.

Next 2 rnds Sc in each st around, changing to CC in last st of last rnd.

Last 2 rnds With CC and working over MC, sc in each st around. Sl st in next st, fasten off.

LARGE BASKET

Work as for medium basket until rnd 17 is completed.

Rnd 18 * Sc in next 5 sts, work 2 sc in next st; rep from * around—84 sts.

Rnd 19 * Sc in next 6 sts, work 2 sc in next st; rep from * around—96 sts.

Rnd 20 * Sc in next 7 sts, work 2 sc in next st; rep from * around—108 sts.

Rnd 21 Sc in each st around.

Rnd 22 * Sc in next 8 sts, work 2 sc in next st; rep from * around—120 sts.

Rnd 23 * Sc in next 9 sts, work 2 sc in next st; rep from * around—132 sts.

Rnd 24 * Sc in next 10 sts, work 2 sc in next st; rep from * around—144 sts.

Rnd 25 Sc in each st around.

Rnd 26 * Sc in next 11 sts, work 2 sc in next st; rep from * around—156 sts.

Rnd 27 * Sc in next 12 sts, work 2 sc in next st; rep from * around–168 sts.

Rnd 28 * Sc in next 13 sts, work 2 sc in next st; rep from * around—180 sts.

Rnd 29 Sc in each st around.

Beg Chart

Next rnd Work 18-st rep of rnd 1 of chart 10 times. Cont to foll chart in this way to rnd 17.

Next 2 rnds Sc in each st around, changing to CC in last st of last rnd.

Last 2 rnds With CC and working over MC, sc in each st around. Sl st in next st, fasten off.

BLOCKING

Set steam iron on polyester setting. Steam-press baskets on RS and WS using a press cloth, rotating as you iron until blocked to finished measurements. It may helpful to slip the basket over a metal can while pressing on RS.

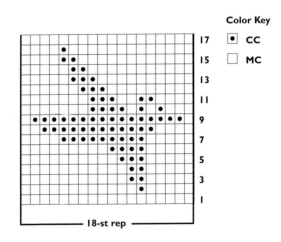

18-st rep

Color Key

⬜ CC

□ MC

CASUAL CLUTCH
Passion flower

Need a clutch that is both casual and fun? Bright and sunny, this Linda Medina design will be the perfect accessory for a spring day.

FINISHED MEASUREMENTS
■ Approx 9"/23cm wide x 5"/12.5cm high

MATERIALS
■ 1 1¾oz/50g skein (approx 175yds/ 160m) each of Koigu *Premium Merino* (wool) in #1013 blue (MC) and #P203 multi (CC)
■ Size D/3 and G/6 (3.25 and 4mm) crochet hooks *or size to obtain gauge*
■ One skein of DMC Six-Strand Embroidery Floss in #3013 light khaki green
■ Sizes 20 and 24 tapestry needles
■ Silver-lined glass "E" beads, 8 each in pink, blue and light green
■ Tissue paper
■ ¼yd/.25m of lining fabric
■ ¼yd/.25m of medium-weight fusible interfacing
■ One ⅞"/22mm button

GAUGE
15 sts and 18 rows to 4"/10cm over sc using 2 strands of yarn held tog and larger hook. *Take time to check gauge.*

Note
Use two strands of yarn held tog throughout unless otherwise stated.

STITCH GLOSSARY
sc2tog [Insert hook into next st and draw up a lp] twice, yo and draw through all 3 lps on hook.

BACK
With 2 strands MC held tog and larger hook, ch 35.
Row 1 Sc in 2nd ch from hook and in each ch across—34 sts. Ch 1, turn.
Rows 2-22 Sc in each st across. Ch 1, turn. When row 22 is completed, do not ch and turn; fasten off.

FRONT
Work as for back.

BOTTOM GUSSET
Work as for back until 4 rows are completed. Fasten off.

SIDE GUSSET
(make 2)
With 2 strands MC held tog and larger hook, ch 5.
Row 1 Sc in 2nd ch from hook and in each ch across—4 sts. Ch 1, turn.
Rows 2-6 Sc in each st across. Ch 1, turn.
Row 7 Sc2tog, sc in last 2 sts—3 sts. Ch 1, turn.
Rows 8-12 Rep row 2.
Rows 13-18 Sc in first 2 sts, sl st in last st. Ch 1, turn. When row 18 is completed, do not ch and turn; fasten off.

BUTTON LOOP
With 1 strand of MC and smaller hook, ch 21.
Row 1 Sl st in 2nd ch from hook and in

each ch across. Fasten off.

Lightly block pieces to measurements.

Embroidery

Trace flower pattern and registration lines onto tissue paper. Baste to front, using registration marks to keep it straight. Work center petals of flowers in chain stitch using one strand of CC. Work outer petals the same way. Using 4 strands of floss, work tendrils in stem stitch. Carefully remove basting and gently tear away tissue. Use 4 strands of floss to sew three beads (one of each color) to center of each flower.

Lining

Measure width of front. Measure height of front and multiply it by 2, then measure depth of bottom gusset and add to the measurement for final length measurement. Cut a piece of lining fabric and interfacing to width and final length measurements. Following manufacturer's instructions, fuse interfacing to WS of lining fabric. Fold lining in half lengthwise, RS facing. Sew side seams using a ¼"/.6cm seam allowance. With WS facing out, square off each corner by folding the corner so point meets side seam; tack in place. Turn top edge ½"/1.3cm to WS and press. Set aside. Using 1 strand of MC, whipstitch bottom edges of side gussets to short edges of bottom gusset. Whipstitch gussets to front and back, then whipstitch remaining open side seams tog (above top edge of side gussets).

Top edging

With RS facing and smaller hook, join 1 strand of MC with a sl st in any side seam.

Rnd 1 Ch 1, making sure that work lies flat, sc evenly around top edge, join rnd with a sl st in first sc.

Rnd 2 Ch 1, working from left to right, sc in each st around. Join rnd with a sl st in first sc. Fasten off. Sew ends of button loop tog, then sew to WS of front so ends are ½"/1.3cm from top edge and loop is centered side to side. Sew button onto back to correspond to button loop. Insert lining. Slipstitch top edge of lining in place.

Embroidery Pattern

FIESTA BAG
Party piñata

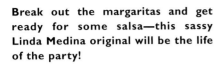

Break out the margaritas and get ready for some salsa—this sassy Linda Medina original will be the life of the party!

FINISHED MEASUREMENTS
▪ Approx 9"/23cm wide x 7½"/19cm high x 3"/7.5cm deep (excluding handle)

MATERIALS
▪ 8 1¾oz/50g balls (each approx 65yds/60m) of Trendsetter Yarns *Swing* (polyamide/tactel nylon/lurex) in #1844 burnt umber (MC) (4)
▪ 2 .7oz/20g balls (each approx 80yds/73m) of Trendsetter Yarns *Eyelash* (polyester) in #78 pumpkin (CC) (4)
▪ Size K/10½ (6.5mm) crochet hook *or size to obtain gauge*
▪ One 7"/17.5cm wide x 6"/15cm high bamboo handle with gold handle clips
▪ One 28yd/26m spool of 10lb test braided beading thread
▪ One 15ft/4.5m package of fine tigertail beading wire
▪ Approx 115 assorted beads and charms
▪ Five or six shank buttons
▪ One package of gold-plated crimp beads
▪ Wire cutters
▪ Crimp pliers
▪ ¼yd/.25m of lining fabric
▪ ¼yd/.25m of medium-weight fusible interfacing
▪ Matching thread

GAUGES
Body of bag
9 sts and 10 rows to 4"/10cm over sc using 3 strands of MC held tog and size K/10½ (6.5mm) hook.
Flap
▪ 10 sts and 10 rows to 4"/10cm over sc using 2 strands of MC, 2 strands of CC, and 1 strand of beading thread held tog and size K/10½ (6.5mm) hook.
Take time to check gauges.

Notes
1 For body of bag, use 3 strands of MC held tog throughout.
2 For flap of bag, use 2 strands of MC, 2 strands of CC, and 1 strand of beading thread held tog throughout.

STITCH GLOSSARY
sc with bead (worked on WS rows) Insert hook into st and draw up a lp. Slide bead (or charm) up to hook, yo and draw through 2 lps on hook.

FRONT
With 3 strands of MC held tog, loosely ch 21.
Row 1 (WS) Sc in 2nd ch from hook and in each ch across—20 sts. Ch 1, turn.
Rows 2-8 Sc in each st across. Ch 1, turn.
Row 9 Skip first st, sc in each to last 2 sts, skip next st, sc in last st—18 sts. Ch 1, turn.
Rows 10-17 Rep row 2.
Row 18 Rep row 9—16 sts.
Row 19 Rep row 2. Fasten off.

BACK

Work as for front until row 18 is completed. Ch 1, turn.

Attach handle

Row 19 (WS) Hold handle upside down on WS of back. Working over first handle clip, sc in first 3 sts sc in next 12 sts; working over 2nd handle clip, sc in last 3 sts. Fasten off.

SIDE GUSSET

(make 2)

With 3 strands of MC held tog, ch 8.

Row 1 Sc in 2nd ch from hook and in each ch across—7 sts. Ch 1, turn.

Rows 2-8 Sc in each st across. Ch 1, turn.

Row 9 Skip first st, sc in each to last 2 sts, skip next st, sc in last st—5 sts. Ch 1, turn.

Rows 10-17 Rep row 2.

Row 18 Rep row 9—3 sts. Fasten off.

BOTTOM GUSSET

With 3 strands of MC held tog, ch 7.

Row 1 Sc in 2nd ch from hook and in each ch across—6 sts. Ch 1, turn.

Rows 2-22 Sc in each st across. Ch 1, turn. When row 22 is completed, do not ch and turn; fasten off.

FLAP

Thread about 80 beads and charms on beading thread. With 2 strands of MC, 2 strands of CC, and 1 strand beading thread held tog, loosely ch 20.

Row 1 (WS) Sc with bead in 2nd ch from hook, *sc in next ch, sc with bead in next ch; rep from * across—19 sts. Ch 1, turn.

Row 2 Sc in each st across. Ch 1, turn.

Row 3 Sc in first st, *sc with bead in next st, sc in next st; rep from * across. Ch 1, turn.

Row 4 Rep row 2.

Row 5 Sc with bead in first st, *sc in next st, sc with bead in next st; rep from * across. Ch 1, turn.

Row 6 Skip first st, sc in each to last 2 sts, skip next st, sc in last st—17 sts. Ch 1, turn.

Row 7 Rep row 3.

Row 8 Rep row 2.

Row 9 Rep row 5.

Row 10 Rep row 2.

Row 11 Rep row 3.

Do not ch, turn. Discontinue beading.

Row 12 Sl st across first 3 sts, work across to last 3 sts. Ch 1, turn—11 sts.

Row 13 Rep row 2. Fasten off.

FINISHING

Lining

Using front, back, side, and bottom gussets as patterns, cut one of each from lining fabric and interfacing; do not add seam allowance. Fuse interfacing following manufacturer's instructions. With RS facing and using a ¼"/.6cm seam allowance, sew lining pieces tog. Fold top edge ⅜"/1cm to WS and press. Set aside.

Using 1 strand of MC, whipstitch bottom edges of side gussets to short edges of bottom gusset. Whipstitch gussets to front and back. Position flap between handle and whipstitch in place. Insert lining. Slipstitch top edge of lining in place.

BEADED FRINGE

Using wire cutters, cut one 12"/30.5cm length of tigertail for each button. Thread button onto tigertail, then one crimp bead. Insert tigertail back up through crimp bead for 1"/2.5cm. Using crimp pliers, crimp the crimp bead. Thread on enough beads to make a 2½"/6.5cm to 3½"/9cm long fringe. Thread on another crimp bead. Beg at bottom right corner of flap, insert end of tigertail through first row of sts. Insert tigertail back through crimp bead and a couple of beads. Pull tight to remove any slack. Use pliers to crimp bead; trim off excess tigertail. Attach next fringe at bottom left corner, then space the remaining fringe evenly between.

SHOULDER BAG
Layer cake

You'll feel pretty in pink (and purple!) carrying this delightful striped shoulder bag by Lisa Pflug.

FINISHED MEASUREMENTS

▥ Approx 11"/28cm wide x 10½"/26.5cm high (excluding strap)

MATERIALS

▥ 16oz/170g skein (each approx 602yd/167m) of Lion Brand Yarn *Homespun* (acrylic/polyester) each in #379 cobalt (A), #392 cotton candy (B), and #386 grape (C) (5)

▥ 1 1¾oz/50g ball (approx 82yd/75m) of Lion Brand Yarn *Moonlight Mohair* (mohair/acrylic/cotton/polyester metallic blend) in #210 painted desert (D) (5)

▥ Size J/9 (5.5mm) crochet hook *or size to obtain gauge*

GAUGE

11 sts and 3 rows to 4"/10cm over hdc using size J/9 (5.5mm) hook.
Take time to check gauge.

Notes

1 To join yarn with a sc, make a slip knot and place on hook. Insert hook into st, yo and draw up a lp, yo and draw through 2 lps on hook.

2 To join yarn with a hdc, make a slip knot and place on hook. Yo, insert hook into st, yo and draw up a lp, yo and draw through all 3 lps on hook.

STITCH GLOSSARY

sc2tog [Insert hook into next st and draw up a lp] twice, yo and draw through all 3 lps on hook.

BACK

With A, ch 24.

Row 1 (RS) Hdc in 3rd ch from hook and in each ch across—22 sts. Fasten off.

Row 2 From RS, join B with a sc in first st, sc in same st, sc in each st across to last st, work 2 sc in last st—24 sts. Fasten off.

Row 3 From RS, join C with a hdc in first st, hdc in same st, hdc in each st across to last st, work 2 hdc in last st—26 sts. Fasten off.

Row 4 From RS, join D with a sc in first st, sc in same st, sc in each st across to last st, work 2 sc in last st—28 sts. Ch 1, turn.

Row 5 Sc in each st across. Ch 1, turn.

Row 6 Rep row 5. Fasten off.

Row 7 From RS, join A with a hdc in first st, hdc in each st across. Fasten off.

Row 8 From RS, join B with a sc in first st, sc in each st across. Fasten off.

Row 9 From RS, join C with a hdc in first st, hdc in each st across. Fasten off.

Rows 10-12 Rep rows 4-6.

Rows 13-24 Rep rows 7-12 twice more. Fasten off.

FRONT

Work as for back.

With A, sc front and back tog.

Top edging

With RS facing, join A with a sl st in any side seam. **Rnd 1** Ch 1, making sure that, work lies flat, sc evenly around top edge, join rnd with a sl st in first sc. **Rnd 2** Ch 1, sc in each st around, join rnd with a sl st in first sc. Fasten off.

Clasp

Locate 6 sts at center of back top edging. **Row 1** Join A with a sc in first of these 6 sts, then sc in next 5 sts—6 sts. Ch 1, turn. **Row 2** Sc in each st across. Ch 1, turn. **Row 3** Sc2tog, sc in next 2 sts, sc2tog—4 sts. Ch 1, turn. **Row 4** Sc2tog, ch 9 for button loop, sc2tog. Fasten off.

Tassel

Using D, make one 4"/10cm-long tassel. Sew to button loop.

Button

With B, ch 2. **Rnd 1** Work 3 sc in 2nd ch from hook, join rnd with a sl st. **Rnd 2** Ch 1, st in each st around, join rnd with a sl st. Fasten off, leaving a long tail. Thread tail in tapestry needle and weave through sts. Wind B into a tight ball the same size as the button. Stuff ball into button, pull tail tight to gather, fasten off securely. Sew on button to correspond to button loop.

Strap

Using three 12yd/11m strands of A held together, join with a sl st to top of any side edge, ch 80, join with a sl st to opposite side edge. Fasten off. To remove stretchiness in handle, stretch handle over an ironing board and lightly steam.

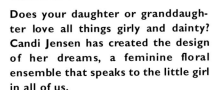

Does your daughter or granddaughter love all things girly and dainty? Candi Jensen has created the design of her dreams, a feminine floral ensemble that speaks to the little girl in all of us.

FINISHED MEASUREMENTS
■ Approx 7"/17.5cm wide x 5½"/14cm high (excluding handle)

MATERIALS
■ 1 3.5oz/99g balls (each approx 198yds/181m) of Coats & Clark (100% acrylic) each in #584 lavender (A), #622 pale sage (B) and #3 off white (C) (4)
■ Size F/5 (3.75mm) crochet hook *or size to obtain gauge*

GAUGE
18 sts and 20 rows to 4"/10cm over sc using size F/5 (3.75mm) hook.
Take time to check gauge.

Note
When changing colors, draw new color through last 2 lps on hook to complete last st.

BACK
Beg at top edge with A, ch 4. Join ch with a sl st, forming a ring. Ch 1, turn.
Row 1 (WS) Work 6 sc in ring. Ch 1, turn.
Row 2 Work 2 sc in each st across—12 sts. Ch 1, turn.
Row 3 Sc in each st across. Ch 1, turn.
Row 4 *Work 2 sc in next st, sc in next st; rep from * across—18 sts. Ch 1, turn.
Row 5 Rep row 2.
Row 6 *Sc in next st, work 2 sc in next st; rep from * across—27 sts. Ch 2, turn.
Row 7 Hdc in each st across, changing to B. Ch 1, turn.
Row 8 Working through back lps only, *work 2 sc in next st, sc in next 2 sts; rep from * across—36 sts. Ch 1, turn.
Row 9 Sc in each st across. Ch 2, turn.
Row 10 Hdc in each st across. Ch 1, turn.
Rows 11-14 Rep row 9, changing to C at the end of row 14. Ch 1, turn.

FLOWER TRIM
Row 15 Sc in first 2 sts, ch 2, *sc in next 4 sts, ch 2; rep from * across, end sc in last 2 sts. Ch 1, turn.
Row 16 Sc in first 2 sts, *in next ch-2 sp work (dc, 3 tr, ch-3, sc in 3rd ch from hook, 3 tr, dc, sc, changing to A)—leaf made. With A, ch 9, work 4 dc in 4th ch from hook, work 4 dc in each of next 5 ch, sc in last ch, changing to C—posie made. With C, sc in next 4 sts; rep from * 7 times more, end sc in last 2 sts. With C, ch 1, turn.
Row 17-19 Sc in each st across. Ch 1, turn.
Rows 20 Sc in first st, sc2tog, sc to last 3 sts, sc2tog, sc in last st—34 sts. Ch 1, turn. Rep row 20 10 times more—14 sts. Fasten off.

FRONT
Work as for back.

With A, ch 91.

Rnd I Sc in 2nd ch from hook and in each ch across to last ch, work 3 sc in last ch. Turn to bottom lps of foundation ch. Sc in first lp and in each lp to last lp, work 2 sc in last lp, join rnd with a sl st in first sc. Fasten off.

Sew front and back together leaving top edge open.

Edging

With RS facing, join A with a sl st in any side seam. **Rnd I** Ch 1, making sure that work lies flat, sc evenly around top edge, join rnd with a sl st in first sc. Fasten off. Sew ends of straps to side seams.

YOGA BAG

Sunset salutation

Routine doesn't have to be all about hustle and bustle—tune in to your spiritual side with this cosmic felted yoga bag designed by Linda Cyr.

FINISHED MEASUREMENTS
■ Approx 7"/17.5cm wide x 21"/53.5cm long (excluding strap)

MATERIALS
■ 5 1¾oz/50g balls (each approx 88yd/81m) of Nashua Handknits *Wooly Stripes* (wool) in #3 key west (4)
■ Size H/8 (5mm) crochet hook *or size to obtain gauge*
■ Safety pin
■ 1½yds/1.5m of 1"/25mm-wide black nylon webbing
■ 1"/25mm black plastic strap adjuster
■ Thread to match strap
■ Sewing needle or sewing machine

GAUGE
14 sts and 16 rnds to 4"/10cm over sc using size H/8 (5mm) hook before felting.
Take time to check gauge.

YOGA MAT BAG
Ch 2.
Bottom
Rnd 1 Work 6 sc in 2nd ch from hook. Mark last st made with the safety pin. You will be working in a spiral, marking the last st made with the safety pin to indicate end of rnd.
Rnd 2 Work 2 sc in each st around—12 sts.

Rnd 3 *Sc in next st, work 2 sc in next st; rep from * around—18 sts.
Rnd 4 *Sc in next 2 sts, work 2 sc in next st; rep from * around—24 sts.
Rnd 5 *Sc in next 3 sts, work 2 sc in next st; rep from * around—30 sts.
Rnd 6 *Sc in next 4 sts, work 2 sc in next st; rep from * around—36 sts.
Rnd 7 *Sc in next 5 sts, work 2 sc in next st; rep from * around—42 sts.
Rnd 8 *Sc in next 6 sts, work 2 sc in next st; rep from * around—48 sts.
Rnd 9 *Sc in next 7 sts, work 2 sc in next st; rep from * around—54 sts.
Rnd 10 *Sc in next 8 sts, work 2 sc in next st; rep from * around—60 sts.
Rnd 11 *Sc in next 9 sts, work 2 sc in next st; rep from * around—66 sts.
Rnd 12 Sl st in each st around. Mark last rnd.
Sides
Rnd 13 Sc in each st around. Rep rnd 13 until piece measures 23"/58.5cm from marked rnd.
Next rnd (strap loop) Ch 5, sk next 5 sts, sc in next 61 sts.
Last rnd Sc in next 5 ch, sl st in next 61 sts. Fasten off.

FINISHING
Felting
Fill washing machine to low-water setting at a hot temperature. Add ¼ cup of a gentle detergent and 2 Tbs. of baking soda. Add bag and also a pair of jeans to provide abrasion and balanced agitation. Use 15 to 20

minute wash cycle, including cold rinse and spin. Check measurements of bag. If it's still bigger than finished measurements, repeat process with progressively shorter cycles, measuring every few minutes until measurements are achieved. Air-dry or machine-dry on a low setting. Steam block to finished measurements.

Strap

For strap adjuster, cut an 8"/20.5cm length of webbing; set aside. For strap, insert end of remaining webbing through strap lp at top of bag from WS to RS, then pull through 1"/2.5cm. Fold in half, then sew across width to secure. Fold opposite end 1"/2.5cm to RS; sew across width. From RS, insert one end of 8"/20.5cm length of webbing through strap adjuster, then pull through 1¼"/3cm. Fold in half to WS, then sew across width. Fold opposite end 1"/2.5cm to WS; sew across width. Position this end so bottom edge is even with marked rnd (rnd 12) and centered with strap lp. Sew across width over previous stitching, then again close to fold at bottom edge.

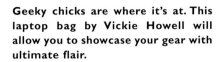

Geeky chicks are where it's at. This laptop bag by Vickie Howell will allow you to showcase your gear with ultimate flair.

FINISHED MEASUREMENTS
▥ Approx 12½"/31.5cm wide x 11"/28cm high x 2"/5cm deep (excluding handles)

MATERIALS
▥ 4 3.5oz/100g skeins (each approx 138yds/126m) of Manos del Uruguay *Manos Multi* stellar **⑤**
▥ Size L/11 (8mm) crochet hook *or size to obtain gauge*
▥ One pair of 9"/23cm diameter round bamboo handles
▥ 1yd/1m of 2½"/65mm wide silk ribbon
▥ Thread to match
▥ Sewing needle

GAUGE
12 sts to 4"/10cm over hdc using size L/11 (8mm) hook before felting.
Take time to check gauge.

Note
Due to the flexibility of the felting process, this bag can be blocked to fit any standard laptop computer.

BACK
Ch 52.
Row 1 Hdc in 3rd ch from hook in each ch across—50 sts. Ch 2, turn.
Row 2 Hdc in each st across. Ch 2, turn. Rep row 2 for pat st and work even until piece measures 12½"/31.5cm from beg. Fasten off.

FRONT
Work as for back.

BOTTOM GUSSET
Work as for bottom until piece measures 2 ½"/6.5 from beg. Fasten off.

SIDE GUSSET
(make 2)
Ch 9.
Row 1 Hdc in 3rd ch from hook in each ch across—7 sts. Ch 2, turn. Rep row 2 as for back until piece measures 12½"/31.5cm from beg. Fasten off.

HANDLE TABS
(make 6)
Ch 13.
Row 1 Hdc in 3rd ch from hook in each ch across—11 sts. Ch 2, turn.
Row 2 Hdc in each st across. Rep row 2 until piece measures 3½"/9cm from beg. Fasten off.

FINISHING
Sew side edges of front and back to side edges of side gussets. Sew bottom gusset to bottom edge of bag. Turn RS out.

Felting
Place bag and handle tabs in a zippered pillowcase cover. Fill washing machine to low-water setting at a hot temperature. Add ¼ cup of a gentle detergent and pillowcase cover. Use 15 to 20-minute wash cycle,

including cold rinse and spin. Check measurements of bag. If it's still bigger than finished or desired measurements, repeat process with progressively shorter cycles, measuring every few minutes until measurements are achieved. Air-dry or machine-dry on a low setting. Steam block to finished measurements.

Ties

Cut ribbon in half. For each tie, turn one cut edge of ribbon ½"/1.3cm to WS; press. Position tie on WS of bag so folded edge is 1"/2.5cm from top edge of bag and centered side to side. Sew in place. Trim ribbon ends in dovetails.

Attaching handles

Position a bamboo handle on front, so one half of it extends beyond top edge of bag and is centered side to side. Pin a handle tab over center bottom of handle, making sure it is centered top to bottom. Sew securely in place along length, just above and below handle. Position second tab, 1¾"/4.5cm to the right and so top right corner is even with top edge of bag; sew in place. Position third tab, 1¾"/4.5cm to the left of center tab and so top left corner is even with top edge of bag; sew in place. Rep on back of bag.

BEADED BAG
Boho fringe

This beaded bag, designed by Margery Winter, is the essence of bohemian romantic.

■ Before felting: 34½"/88cm x 36"/91.5cm
■ After felting: approx 21"/53.5cm x 30"/76cm

MATERIALS

■ 3 1¾oz/50g balls (each approx 120yds/111m) of Berroco, Inc. *Suede* (nylon) in #3717 Wild Bill Hickcock (A) (4)
■ 3 1¾oz/50g balls (each approx 100yds/92m) of Berroco, Inc. *Idol* (cotton/nylon/polyester) in #1517 Diana (B) (4)
■ 1 1¾oz/50g ball (approx 100yds/92m) of Berroco, Inc. *Suede Deluxe* (nylon/rayon/polyester) in #3904 hopalong gold (C) (4)
■ Size G/6 and K/10½ (4 and 6.5mm) crochet hooks *or size to obtain gauge*
■ 1½yd/1.5m of ⅜"/1cm-wide metal link chain in antique gold
■ Large metallic beads in antique gold
■ Large wood beads in black and brown
■ Large gold charms
■ Large jump rings in antique gold
■ Mini metallic brad fasteners in antique gold, pewter, rust, and brown
■ Safety pin

GAUGES

Body of bag
11 sts and 13 rnds to 4"/10cm over sc using 1 strand each of A and C held tog and larger hook.

Flap
22 sts and 18 rows to 4"/10cm over sc pat st using 1 strand C and smaller hook.
Take time to check gauges.

Notes

1 For body of bag, use 1 strand each of A and B held tog throughout.
2 For flap of bag, use 1 strand of C throughout.

BAG

With larger hook and 1 strand each of A and B held tog, ch 52.

Row 1 Sc in 2nd ch from hook and in each ch across—51 sts. Ch 1, turn.

Rows 2-8 Sc in each st across. Ch 1, turn. When row 8 is completed, ch 1, turn to short side edge. You will now be working in rnds.

Rnd 1 Work 8 sc evenly spaced across side edge, turn to bottom lps of foundation ch, sc in each of next 51 lps, turn to side edge, work 8 sc evenly spaced across side edge, turn to top edge, sc in each of next 51 sts—118 sts. Mark last st made with the safety pin. You will be working in a spiral (except for rnd 22), marking the last st made with the safety pin to indicate end of rnd.

Rnds 2-12 Sc in each st around.

Rnd 13 Sc in first 6 sts, [sk next st, sc in next st] 20 times, sc in next 21 sts, [sk next st, sc in next st] 20 times, sc in each st to end—98 sts.

Rnds 14 and 15 Sc in each st around.

Rnd 16 Sc in first 5 sts, [sk next st, sc in next st] 11 times, sc in next 17 sts, [sk next st, sc in next st] 11 times, sc in each st to end—76 sts.

Rnds 17 and 18 Sc in each st around. When rnd 18 is completed, change to C and smaller hook.

Rnds 19-21 Sc in each st around.

Rnd 22 Ch 3 (counts as 1 dc), *ch 1, sk next st, dc in next st; rep from * around, join rnd with a sl st in 3rd ch of beg ch-3.

Rnd 23 Sc in each st and ch-1 sp around.

Rnd 24 Sc in each st around. Sl st in next st. Fasten off.

Flap

Flatten bag so top and side edges are even.

Row 1(RS) Count 1 st from right side edge. With smaller hook, join C with a sl st in next st, ch 1, sc in next 35 sts—35 sts. Ch, 1 turn.

Row 2 and 3 Sc in each st across. Ch 1, turn.

Row 4 Sc in first st, *ch 1, sk next st, sc in next st; rep from *. Ch 1, turn.

Row 5 Sc in first st, *sc in next ch-1 sp, ch 1; rep from *, end sc in last ch-1 sp, sc in last st. Ch 1, turn.

Row 6 Sc in first st, *ch 1, sc in next ch-1 sp; rep from *, end ch 1, sc in last st. Ch 1, turn. Rep rows 5 and 6 for sc pat st until flap measures 5"/12.5cm from beg, end with row 5 (RS row).

Next row (WS) Work across to last 6 sts—29 sts. Ch 1, turn. Work 3 rows even.

Next row (WS) Work across to last 4 sts—25 sts. Ch 1, turn. Work next row even. Rep last 2 rows once more—21sts.

Next row Work across to last 2 sts—19 sts. Ch 1, turn. Rep last row 5 times more—9 sts.

Fasten off.

Handle

Cut 16 36"/91.5cm strands of each color. Gather strands tog, mixing colors. Make a knot 4"/10cm from one end for first tassel. Divide strands into 3 groups of 16 strands. Braid for 22"/56cm, then knot end for second tassel. Trim tassels 3 ½"/9cm long. Fold up one end of chain 6"/15cm and attach links together with a jump ring. Weave chain through handle, beg and ending above tassel knots. To attach handle, position top edge of knots just below first C rnd (rnd 19) of bag. Sew handle in place each side from bottom edge of knot to top edge of bag. Decorate chain with charms, single beads, or strands of multiple beads strung onto and attached with C.

Fringe

Cut 9"/23cm strands of C. Using 2 strands for each fringe, attach 1 fringe to each st and row along entire edge of flap. Trim ends. Decorate flap with mini metallic brad fasteners as desired.

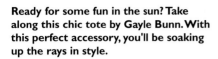

Ready for some fun in the sun? Take along this chic tote by Gayle Bunn. With this perfect accessory, you'll be soaking up the rays in style.

FINISHED MEASUREMENTS

▓ Approx 11½"/29cm wide x 12"/30.5cm high (excluding straps)

MATERIALS

▓ 2 3½oz/100g hanks (each approx 100yds) of Classic Elite Yarns *Provence* (cotton) in #2661 summer wheat (D) ③
▓ 1 hank each in #2616 natural (A), #2619 zinnia flower (B), and #2633 sun-drenched yellow (C)
▓ Size H/8 (5mm) crochet hook *or size to obtain gauge*
▓ ½yd/.5m of lining fabric
▓ Matching thread

GAUGE

7 clusters and 13 rows to 4"/10, over pat st using size H/8 (5mm) hook.
Take time to check gauge.

Note

When working stripe sequence, join new color at beg of rnd as foll: sl st in next hdc, then sl st in sp between clusters, drawing new color through this 2nd sl st.

TOTE

Beg at bottom; with A, ch 37.

Rnd 1 Sc in 2nd ch from hook, sc in next 34 ch, work 2 sc in last ch, turn to bottom lps of foundation ch, sc in next 35 lps, work 2 sc in last lp, join rnd with a sl st in first sc.

Rnd 2 Ch 1, sc in same st as joining, sc in next 35 sts, work 3 sc in next st, sc in next 36 sts, work 3 sc in next sc, join rnd with a sl st in first st.

Rnd 3 Ch 1, sc in same st as joining, sc in next 36 sts, work 3 sc in next st, sc in next 38 sts, work 3 sc in next st, sc in next st, join rnd with a sl st in first sc—82 sts.

Beg pat st

Rnd 1 Ch 2 (counts as 1 hdc), hdc in same sp as last sl st (beg cluster made), *skip next st, work 2 hdc (cluster) in back lp of next st; rep from * around to last st, skip last st, join rnd with a sl st in 2nd ch of beg ch-2—41 cluster sts.

Rnd 2 Sl st in next hdc and sp between clusters, ch 2, hdc in same sp as last sl st, *work cluster in sp between last cluster and next cluster; rep from * around, join rnd with a sl st in 2nd ch of beg ch-2. Rep rnd 2 for pat st and cont in stripe sequence as foll: 13 rnds A, 4 rnds B, 4 rnds C, and 16 rnds D.

Next rnd Ch 1, sc in each hdc around, join rnd with a sl st in first sc.

Last rnd Ch 1, working from left to right, sc in each st around, join rnd with a sl st in first st. Fasten off.

STRAP

(make 2)

With D, ch 123.

Row 1 (WS) Sc in 2nd ch from hook and in each ch across—122 sts. Ch 1, turn.

Rows 2-4 Sc in each sc across. Ch 1, turn. When row 4 is completed, ch 1, do not turn.

Edging

Rnd 1 (RS) Working from left to right, sc in each st (or bottom lp of foundation ch) around, join rnd with a sl st in first sc. Fasten off.

FINISHING

Lining

Cut one 12½"/31.5cm x 24"/61cm strip from fabric. Fold strip in half lengthwise. Using a ½"/1.3cm seam allowance throughout, sew seam. Press seam open. With RS together, position seam in center; press. Sew bottom seam. Sew diagonally across bottom corner, 1"/2.5cm from corner. Trim bottom and corner seams to ¼"/.5cm. Insert lining into bag. Turn top edge to WS so top edge of lining is ¾"/2cm from top edge of tote. Remove from tote, press top edge and set aside. Position each end of strap so outer edge is 2"/5cm from side edge of tote and bottom edge is 2"/5cm from top edge of tote. Sew in place. Insert lining. Slipstitch top edge of lining in place.

Tote of many colors

in this design Sasha Kagan crochets a simple striped circle, which when folded in half creates this visually stunning tote. Adjust the diameter to make this a bag for any occasion.

FINISHED MEASUREMENTS
■ Approx 21"/53.5cm wide x 9½"/24cm high (excluding handle)

MATERIALS
■ 1 1¾oz/50g ball (each approx 186yd/170m) of Rowan/Westminster Fibers, Inc. *4 Ply Cotton* (cotton) each in #136 bluebell (A), #137 cooking apple (B), #135 fennel (C), #130 ardour (D), #120 orchid (E), #133 cheeky (F), #132 bloom (G), and #138 tutti frutti (H) 1
■ Size 4 (2mm) steel crochet hook *or size to obtain gauge*
■ One 9¾"/24.5cm wide x 6"/15cm high D-shaped bamboo handle by Rowan

GAUGE
28 sts and 29 rnds to 4"/10cm over sc using size 4 (2mm) steel hook.
Take time to check gauge.

Notes
1 When changing colors, draw new color through sl st when joining rnd.
2 Do not carry up colors; cut and join them as needed.

STITCH GLOSSARY
sc2tog [Insert hook into next st and draw up a lp] twice, yo and draw through all 3 lps on hook.

BAG
With A, ch 4. Join ch with a sl st, forming a ring.
Rnd 1 Work 8 sc in ring, join rnd with a sl st in first sc, changing to B.
Rnd 2 Ch 1, work 2 sc in each st around, join rnd with a sl st in first sc, changing to C—16 sts.
Rnd 3 Ch 1, *sc in next st, work 2 sc in next st; rep from * around, join rnd with a sl st in first sc, changing to D—24 sts.
Rnd 4 Ch 1, sc in each st around, join rnd with a sl st in first sc, changing to E.
Rnd 5 Ch 1, *sc in next st, work 2 sc in next st; rep from * around, join rnd with a sl st in first sc, changing to F—36 sts.
Rnd 6 Ch 1, sc in each st around, join rnd with a sl st in first sc, changing to G.
Rnd 7 Ch 1, *sc in next 2 sts, work 2 sc in next st; rep from * around, join rnd with a sl st in first sc, changing to H—48 sts.
Rnd 8 Ch 1, sc in each st around, join rnd with a sl st in first sc, changing to G.
Rnd 9 Ch 1, *sc in next 3 sts, work 2 sc in next st; rep from * around, join rnd with a sl st in first sc, changing to F—60 sts.
Rnd 10 Ch 1, sc in each st around, join rnd with a sl st in first sc, changing to E.
Rnd 11 Ch 1, *sc in next 4 sts, work 2 sc in

next st; rep from * around, join rnd with a sl st in first sc, changing to D—72 sts.

Rnd 12 Ch 1, sc in each st around, join rnd with a sl st in first sc, changing to C.

Rnd 13 Ch 1, *sc in next 5 sts, work 2 sc in next st; rep from * around, join rnd with a sl st in first sc changing to B—84 sts.

Rnd 14 Ch 1, sc in each st around, join rnd with a sl st in first sc, changing to A. Cont to inc 12 sts every other rnd by working 1 more st between incs. AT THE SAME TIME, cont to work in stripe sequence as foll: *1 rnd each A, B, C, D, E, F, G, H, G, F, E, D, C, and B; rep * (14 rnds) for stripe sequence. Work until piece measures 21"/53.5cm in diameter.

Button loop

Row 1 Ch 12, sk next 6 sts, join yarn with a sl st in next st. Do not ch, turn.

Row 2 Sl st in each ch across. Fasten off. This side is the back of the bag.

FINISHING

Fold circle in half so button loop is at center top. Sew an 8"/20.5cm seam each side. Fold front top edge over crossbar of handle to WS; sew in place.

Button

With G, ch 3. Join ch with a sl st, forming a ring.

Rnd 1 Work 8 sc in ring, join rnd with a sl st in first sc.

Rnd 2 Ch 1, *sc in next st, work 2 sc in next st; rep from * around, join rnd with a sl st in first st—12 sts.

Rnds 3 and 4 Ch 1, sc in each st around, join rnd with a sl st in first st.

Rnd 5 Ch 1, [sc2tog] 6 times—6 sts. Fasten off, leaving a long tail. Thread tail in tapestry needle and weave through sts. Wind G into a tight ball the same size as the button. Stuff ball into button, pull tail tight to gather, fasten off securely. Sew on button to correspond to button loop.

TEAL RUFFLE BAG

Aqua marine

Whether you are a lover of the sea or clear skies, you can't help but see the beauty in a deep aqua blue. Let that beauty imbue your outfit with this fantastic ruffle bag designed by Elena Malo.

■ Approx 8"/20.5cm wide x 5"/12.5cm high (excluding strap)

■ 4 1¾oz/50g balls (each approx 98yds/ 90m) of Karabella *Zodiac* (cotton) in #481 turquoise ▮4▮
■ Size G/6 (4mm) crochet hook *or size to obtain gauge*
■ ¼yd/.25m of lining fabric
■ Matching thread
■ One 1⅜"/34mm button

18 sts to 4"/10cm over ruffle pat using size G/6 (4mm) hook.
Take time to check gauge.

MP (make picot) Ch 3, sl st in 3rd ch from hook.

Ch 35.
Row I Sc in 2nd ch from hook and in each ch across—34 sts. Ch 3, turn.
Row 2 Dc in each st across. Ch 1, turn.
Row 3 Sc in each st across. Ch 7, turn.
Row 4 Sl st in 3rd ch from hook (first picot made), tr in back lp of first sc, MP, *work (tr, MP, tr) in back lp of next sc; rep from * to last sc, work (tr, MP, ch 4, sl st) in back lp of last sc. Ch 1, turn.
Row 5 Sc in back (free) lp of each sc of row 3. Ch 3, turn. Rep rows 2-5 4 times more, then rows 2 and 3 once. Ch 7, turn.
Next row Sl st in 3rd ch from hook (first picot made), tr in back lp of first sc, MP, [work (tr, MP, tr) in back lp of next sc] 13 times. Fasten off. Skip 6 center sts, join yarn with a sl st in back lp of next st, ch 7. Sl st in 3rd ch from hook (first picot made), tr in back lp of same sc as joining, MP, [work (tr, MP, tr) in back lp of next sc] 12 times, work (tr, MP, ch 4, sl st) in back lp of last sc. Ch 1, turn.
Last row Rep row 5, working through back (free) lps of row 3 and through both lps of 6 center sts. Fasten off.

Ch 101.
Row I Sc in 2nd ch from hook and in each ch across. Ch 3, turn.
Row 2 Dc in each st across. Ch 1, turn.
Row 3 Sc in each st across. Fasten off.

Ch 21.
Row I Sc in 2nd ch from hook and in each ch across. Fasten off.

Lining
Measure, mark, and cut out two pieces of lining ½"/1.3cm larger all around than bag.

allowance, sew pieces tog along side and bottom edges. Turn top edge ½"/1.3cm to WS and press. Sew side and bottom seams of bag together. Pin button lp to back of bag, so bottom edges of lp are side by side, ½"/1.3cm from top edge and centered side to side; sew in place. Sew ends of strap to top side edges of bag. Sew on button to correspond to button lp. Insert lining. Slipstitch top edge of lining in place.

CINCHED STRETCH BAG
Vertigo vision spiral

Disco fever! Designed by Elena Malo, this cinched spiral stitch bag has the same flash and flair as the mirrored disco balls of yesteryear.

FINISHED MEASUREMENTS

■ Approx 10½"/26.5cm wide x 10"/25.5cm high (excluding handles)

MATERIALS

■ 2 1¾oz/50g balls (each approx 262yds/240m) of Tahki Yarns/Tahki•Stacy Charles, Inc. *Dream* (wool/nylon) each in #3 spring green (A), #13 purple haze (B) and #4 pink (C) (**4**)

■ Size G/6 (4mm) crochet hook *or size to obtain gauge*

■ One pair of 5½"/14cm wide x 4½"/11.5cm high U-shaped bamboo handles with gold clips

■ ½yd/.5m of lining fabric

■ Matching thread

GAUGE

11 sts and 8 rnds to 4"/10cm over spiral pat using 2 strands of yarn held tog and size G/6 (4mm) hook.

Take time to check gauge.

Notes

1 Use 2 strands of yarn held tog throughout.
2 When changing colors, draw new color through last 2 lps on hook to complete last BPDC
3 It is not necessary to mark the beg of rnds because it will be dictated by spiral pat and stripes.

STITCH GLOSSARY

FPDC (front post dc) Yo, working from front to back to front, insert hook around post of st of rnd below, yo and draw up a lp, [yo and draw through 2 lps on hook] twice.

BPDC (back post dc) Yo, working from back to front to back, insert hook around post of st of rnd below, yo and draw up a lp, [yo and draw through 2 lps on hook] twice.

BAG

With 2 strands of A held tog, ch 3. Join ch with a sl st, forming a ring.

Rnd 1 Ch 1, work 10 sc in ring, join rnd with a sl st in beg ch.

Rnd 2 Ch 1, work 2 sc in each st around, join rnd with a sl st in first st—20 sts.

Rnd 3 Ch 1, *sc in next st, work 2 sc in next st; rep from * around, join rnd with a sl st in first st—30 sts. From here on, work in continuous rnds without joining.

Rnd 4 Ch 3, *dc in next 2 sts, work 2 dc in next st; rep from * 9 times more—40 sts.

Beg spiral pat

Rnd 5 *FPDC around each of next 2 sts, dc in space between last and next dc (inc 1 st made), BPDC around each of next 2 sts, inc 1 st; rep from * around—you should have 10 sections each of FPDC and BPDC, end BPDC around first FPDC.

Rnd 6 *FPDC around each of next 2 sts, inc 1 st, FPDC around first BPDC, BPDC around each of next 2 sts, inc 1 st, BPDC around next FPDC; rep from * around end BPDC around first FPDC of previous rnd.

Rnds 7 and 8 Rep rnd 6—120 sts. AT SAME TIME, when rnd 8 is completed, change to 2 strands of B. Cont to work in pat as established moving pat 1 st to the left every rnd and working stripe sequence as foll: *4 rnds B, 4 rnds C, 4 rnds A; rep from * once more, then work 4 rnds B and 4 rnds C, changing to A.

Edging

Rnd 1 Ch 3, *yo, working from back to front to back, insert hook around and under top lps of st below, yo and draw up a lp, [yo and draw through 2 lps on hook] twice; rep from * around, join rnd with a sl st in first st.

Rnd 2 (eyelets) Ch 4 (counts as 1 dc and ch 1), *skip next st, dc in next st, ch 1; rep from * around, join rnd with a sl st in 3rd ch of beg ch-4.

Rnd 3 Ch 1, sc in each st and ch-1 sp around, join rnd with a sl st in first st.

Rnds 4 and 5 Ch 1, working through back lps only, sc in each st around, join rnd with a sl st in first sc. When rnd 5 is completed, fasten off.

Lining

Cut one 9½"/24cm x 23"/58.5cm strip and one 7½"/19cm-diameter circle. Fold strip in half lengthwise. Sew side seam using a ½"/1.3cm seam, forming a tube. Around one end of tube, make ⅜"/1cm deep clips about ½"/1.3cm apart. With RS facing, pin clipped end of tube to circle, spreading out fabric tabs. Sew seam using a ½"/1.3cm seam allowance. Trim all seams ¼"/.5cm. Test fit into bag, turning top edge over to WS so top edge is even with top of rnd 1 of edging; remove and press turnover. Slipstitch top edge of lining in place. On WS, use A to whipstitch each handle clip in place, making sure that bottom edge of clip is even with top edge of eyelet rnd.

Twisted cord drawstring (make 2)

Cut four 90"/228.5cm strands of A. Put strands together and fold in half. Tie ends into a knot. Holding the knot in your hand, slip the loop over a hook and pull tight. Slip a pencil through the knotted end, then rotate the pencil, twisting the cord until it starts to double back on itself. Put one finger in center of cord and carefully fold in half, letting two ends of cord twist together. Make a knot 1"/2.5cm from each end, trim off ends ¼"/.5cm from base of knots. Weave one drawstring through eyelets across front edging and one through eyelets across back edging. Tie ends into bows on each side.

RUFFLE TIER BAG
Prim and proper

Crocheted bags may be fun and trendy, but they can also be delicate and elegant. This scalloped Doris Chan bag would be an ideal complement to any formal attire.

KNITTED MEASUREMENTS

■ 6½"/16.5cm wide x 8"/20.5cm high x 2"/5cm deep, not including 4½"/11.5cm in diameter handles

MATERIALS
■ 4 1¾oz/50g balls (each approx 191yd/175m) of Coats & Clark *Opera* (No. 5 crochet cotton) in #502 cream ⑤
■ Size F/5 (3.75 mm) crochet hook
■ Size D/3 (3.25 mm) crochet hook
■ Size 13 or 14 steel crochet hook for beading
■ 6mm round pearl beads in cream/ivory, 70 beads (optional)
■ Two lids from small coffee cans or similar lids, 4"/10cm diameter
■ Curved nail scissors or sharp pointed craft scissors
■ Emery board or fine sandpaper
■ Scrap of yarn for marker

GAUGES
20 sts and 22 rows = 4"/10cm over sc with double strand of thread using F/5 (3.75mm) hook.
4 rows of trim pat = approx 1¾"/4.5cm with single strand of thread using D/3 (3.25mm) hook (exact gauge not critical).
Take time to check gauges.

STITCHES
FPSC (front post single crochet)
Insert hook from front to back around post of specified sc.

HANDLES
Prepare plastic rounds for handles as foll:
Start with two clean lids and curved, sharp nail scissors. Cut out and remove flat center part of lid, leaving a ¼"/6mm-wide inner ridge and the outer rim (the part that snaps over the edge of the can). Sand away any rough spots with emery board.
With F-5 (3.75 mm) hook, 4 strands of thread held tog as one, and outer rim facing toward you, join thread to ring with a sl st worked through center of one ring (hold lp on hook outside ring, insert hook into center of ring and yo, draw through lp on hook), ch 1, cover ring with approx 80 sc evenly spaced around, join with sl st to first sc. Fasten off. Rep with rem ring.

BAG
Notes
1 Body of bag is worked with 2 strands of thread held tog as one.
2 Join end of each rnd with sl st in first sc.
3 Do not count joining sl sts as a st; do not work into sl sts.

BASE
Rnd 1 (WS) With F/5 (3.75 mm) hook, ch 30, starting in 2nd ch from hook, sc in each of next 28 ch, 3 sc in last ch; working along opposite edge of foundation ch, sc in each of next 27 ch, 2 sc in same ch as first sc,

join—60 sc. Ch 1, turn.

Rnd 2 Ch 1, work 2 sc in each of next 2 sc, sc in each of next 27 sc, 2 sc in each of next 3 sc, sc in each of next 27 sc, 2 sc in last sc, join —66 sc. Ch 1, turn.

Rnd 3 Ch 1, work 2 sc in next sc, sc in each of next 28 sc, (2 sc in next sc, sc in next sc) twice, 2 sc in next sc, sc in each of next 28 sc, 2 sc in next sc, sc in next sc, 2 sc in next sc, sc in last sc, join—72 sc. Ch 1, turn.

Rnd 4 Ch 1, sc in next sc, 2 sc in next sc, sc in each of next 2 sc, 2 sc in next sc, sc in each of next 29 sc, (2 sc in next sc, sc in next 2 sc) twice, 2 sc in next sc, sc in each of next 29 sc, 2 sc in next sc, sc in last sc, join—78 sc. Ch 1, turn.

Rnd 5 Ch 1, sc in next each of next 2 sc, 2 sc in next sc, sc in each of next 30 sc, (2 sc in next sc, sc in each of next 3 sc) twice, 2 sc in next sc, sc in each of next 30 sc, 2 sc in next sc, sc in each of next 3 sc, 2 sc in next sc, sc in last sc, join—84 sc. Fasten off.

BODY
Sides

Rnd 1 (WS) With double strand of thread, F/5 (3.75 mm) hook and WS of base facing, sk joining sl st and next 2 sc, join with sl st around next front post of next sc, ch 1, work FPSC around each of next 84 sc, join with sl st in first sc—joining is now positioned at one side of bag. Ch 1, turn.

Rnds 2-7 (work even) Sc in each of 84 sc around, join with sl st in first sc. Ch 1, turn.

Rnd 8 (foundation rnd for trim) Sc in next sc, [ch 1, sk next sc, sc in each of next 2 sc] 27 times, ch 1, sk next sc, sc in last sc, join with sl st to first sc—28 ch-1 spaces and 28 sk sc. Ch 1, turn.

Rnd 9 Sc in next sc, [sc in next ch-1 sp, sc in each of next 2 sc] 27 times, sc in next ch-1 sp, sc in last sc, join with sl st to first sc—84 sc. Ch 1, turn.

Rnds 10-41 Repeat rnds 2-9 4 times more. Fasten off.

BEADED TRIM
Note

1 Work in joined rnds, with RS facing.

2 Work with single strand of thread.

3 To join beads (sl bead), drop lp from D hook. Sl one bead onto steel hook. Insert steel hook into dropped lp. Keeping work tight, draw lp through bead, drawing up lp to accommodate D hook. Re-insert D hook into lp, tighten, and cont.

TIER 1

Hold bag upside down.

Rnd 1 With single strand of thread and D/3 (3.25mm) hook, join thread with sl st in first sk sc on rnd 7 of bag after joining st, ch 1, sc in same sc, [ch 3, sc in next sk sc] 27 times, ch 1, hdc in first sc—28 ch-3 lps, counting last ch-1 and hdc as 1 lp.

Rnd 2 Sl st in last lp made, ch 3, dc in same lp, [ch 2, 5 sc in next ch-3 lp, ch 2, work (2 dc, ch 2, 2 dc—shell made) in next ch-3 lp] 13 times, ch 2, 5 sc in next ch-3 lp, ch 2, 2 dc in first lp, ch 1, sc in 3rd ch of starting ch-3—14 shells, counting last ch-1 and sc as 1 space.

Rnd 3 Sl st in last space made, ch 3, 2 dc in same space, [ch 3, skip next sc, sc in each of next 3 sc, ch 3, work (3 dc, ch 2, 3 dc) in ch-2 space of next shell] 13 times, ch 3, sk next sc, sc in each of next 3 sc, ch 3, 3 dc in first space, ch 1, sc in top of third ch of starting ch-3. Fasten off for beading rnd.

Note

To work without beads, work shells of rnd 4 as foll: (4 dc, ch 2, 4 dc) in ch-2 space of previous rnd.

Rnd 4 (beading rnd) Sl st in last space made, ch 3, 3 dc in same space, [ch 4, skip next sc, sc in next sc, ch 4, work (4 dc, sl bead, ch 1, 4 dc) in next space] 13 times, ch 4, skp next sc, sc in next sc, ch 4, 4 dc in first space, sl bead, ch 1, sl st in ch of starting ch-3. Fasten off.

TIER 2

Working along rnd 15 of bag, offset the points of the trim by joining thread in first skp sc before joining, work 4 rnds of trim in same way.

TIER 3

Working along rnd 23 of bag, join in first skip sc after joining (align trim with Tier 1), work trim in same way.

TIER 4

Working along rnd 31 of bag, work as for Tier 2.

TIER 5

Working along rnd 39 of bag, work as for Tier 3.

CASING

Row 1 (RS) With F–5 (3.75mm) hook and double strands of thread, hold bag right side up, locate join at center of one side, sk next 8 sc, join with sl st in next sc, ch 1, sc in same sc, sc in each of next 25 sc—26 sc. Ch 1, turn.

Rows 2-10 Ch 1, sc in each across. Ch 1, turn.

Keep last lp on hook, cut thread leaving 18"/45.5cm tail. With RS of handle and casing facing you, fold casing in half to inside of bag through handle, passing hook and tail of thread through center of handle. Turn. With WS facing and matching sts of row 10 of casing to sts of row 1, *insert hook in sc of row 10, insert hook around post of corresponding sc on row 1, work 1 sl st to join the 2 sts; rep from * across. Fasten off.

Make casing and attach handle to other side of bag in same way. Weave in ends. Steam block ruffles, being careful not to melt beads or handles.

The perfect evening is not complete without the perfect bag. Designed by Mari Lynn Patrick, this bag will be the beautiful finishing touch to your special night.

FINISHED MEASUREMENTS
■ 11"/ 28cm wide x 6"/15cm deep

MATERIALS
■ 5 .88oz/25g balls (each approx 132yd/ 120m) of Tahki•Stacy Charles, Inc. Filatura di Crosa *New Smoking* in #4 Copper **(3)**
■ Size G/7 (4.5mm) hook *or size to obtain gauge*
■ Two 1½"/4cm D-rings
■ One 2"/5cm metal buckle or 1½"/4cm brooch

GAUGE
18 sc and 20 rows to 4"/10cm over sc pat using 2 strands of yarn held tog and size G/7 (4.5mm) hook.
Take time to check gauge.

Notes
1 Work with double strand of yarn held tog throughout.
2 Leave long ends of yarn at the top of gusset joinings to reinforce at the top when finishing.

BAG
Note If clutch style is being worked, do not use the D-rings; simply work the gusset.

GUSSET
With double strands of yarn, work sc evenly around one D-ring, join with sl st to first sc, ch 1, turn.
Row 1 Working along the straight edge of the D-ring only, work 8 sc across, ch 1, turn. Cont in sc pat on 8 sc until gusset measures 8½"/21.5cm from D-ring. Fasten off. Work the 2nd D-ring with 8½"/21.5cm gusset in same way then sc the last sc rows of gusset tog from WS to form the bottom center of the bag. The gusset with D-rings attached measures 17"/43cm. Lay work aside.

FRONT
** With double strand of yarn, beg at bottom edge, ch 37.
Row 1 (RS) Work 1 sc in 2nd ch from hook and in each ch to end—36 sc. Turn.
Row 2 Ch 3, sc in 2nd ch from hook and in each ch to end—38 sc. Turn.
Rep row 2 for 5 times more—48 sc. Cont in sc until there are a total of 27 rows from beg **. Do not fasten off. Place a yarn marker at center of beg ch (count 18 sc and pm) for bottom center of bag. Return to top edge and cont around side edge of front, (and working in between each sc or row), work 22 sc to lower edge, 18 sc to marker, 18 sc to end of lower edge, 22 sc around other shaped edge, then sl st firmly across top edge. Cont to sc front and gusset tog from the RS and matching up the marker to lower center of gusset, work 1 sc in each sc of front tog through the gusset. Fasten off.

BACK

Work as for front from ** to **.

Next row (WS) Work 20 sc, work 8 next sc through front lps only (for tab), work 20 sc. Work even for 2"/5cm or 10 rows more.

FLAP SHAPING

Next row (RS) Pull up a lp in each of first 2 sc, yo and through all 3 lps (for dec 1 sc), sc to last 2 sc, dec 1 sc. Ch 1, turn.

Rep the last row 3 times more. Fasten off. From RS, with 2 strands of yarn, work 66 sc evenly around the flap, then place yarn marker between the 36 sc along the lower edge and join gusset to the back in same way (be sure to eliminate the flap).

BUCKLE TAB

From RS, join 2 strands of yarn and work 8 sc into the center free lps at beg of the flap. Work 18 rows even in sc. Dec 1 sc each side of next 2 rows. Fasten off the rem 4 sc.

STRAP

Join 2 strands of yarn with sl st to top of D-ring and work 5 sc across, then ch 100 for one side of strap; then, being careful not to twist ch; work 5 sc across opposite D-ring and ch100; for other side of strap, * join to first of the 5 sc on the first D-ring, ch 1, work 2 sc in first of the 5 sc then working along the 100 ch, work 1 hdc in each ch, join; rep from * on the opposite D-ring and ch. To join both lengths of 100 hdc, work 1 sc in D-ring then from RS, work sc through both sets of 100 hdc to join the 2 chains and create a ridge on the RS, join and sc into the center sc of opposite ring.

FINISHING

Use strands left at top of bag under the flap to reinforce the bag along the D-ring fastenings. Stuff bag with tissue paper and steam lightly to give bag its shape. Trim tab with buckle or brooch.

■■■■

Feeling a little wild? Embrace your primal passions in this freeform design by Noreen Crone-Findlay.

FINISHED MEASUREMENTS

■ Approx 13"/33cm wide x 7½"/19cm high x 4"/10cm deep (excluding handles and fringe)

MATERIALS

■ 1 1¾oz/50g ball (each approx 55yd/50m) of S.R. Kertzer *Baby Monkey* (polyamide) each in #160 fuchsia (A) and #210 purple (B) **④**

■ 2 1¾/50g balls (each approx 109yd/100m) of Stylecraft *Marrakech* (nylon/acrylic) in #1152 delight (C) **③**

■ 1 3½oz/100g skein (approx 220yd/200m) of S.R. Kertzer *Super 10* (cotton) in #2006 midnight (D) **③**

■ Size H/8 (5mm) crochet hook

■ Large spool knitter (approx 2½"/6cm in diameter) by Crone-Findlay

■ One 12½"/31.5cm x 8"/20.5cm x 4"/10cm plastic mesh bag frame TM22 from Lacis

■ One 12oz/343g 'Mass 0' Glass' tub of beads from Michaels Arts and Crafts

■ 2yds/2m of 26-gauge copper wire

■ Wire cutters

■ Needle nose pliers

GAUGE

No gauge requirement is needed.

MESH BAG FOUNDATION

To make first of two double-layer handles, first cut across top edge of front half of mesh bag, following the first straight line (7 squares down from upper point of side edge and 3 squares down from upper edge at center). Cut a strip that is 2 mesh wide x 39 mesh long. Trim edges smooth. Cut another strip the same size. Trim top edge of bag smooth. Rep on back half of bag.

Marking pieces

Fasten a yarn marker to center top mesh on front and back bag halves. On each half, count 8 mesh in from each top side edge and fasten a yarn marker in the 9th mesh.

Attaching handles

Place 2 handle strips tog. At top edge of front bag half, position first handle so inner edges are 4 mesh from marked center mesh and ends of handles overlap top edge by 2 mesh; pin in place. Stitch ends in place securely using A. Rep on back bag half. Remove these markers.

Assembling bag

Overlap one side of the bag over the other, matching 9th mesh yarn markers. Using A, stitch through both 9th mesh to secure the sides together, then whipstitch each of the loose edges to the bag. Cont to whipstitch edges together working down side edges of bag, then across to center bottom edges; fasten off. Rep on opposite side edges.

Cover bag with chain stitch crochet as foll: With 1 strand each of A and C (or B and C) held tog, make a slip knot. Hold slip knot on WS of bag. From RS, insert hook into mesh and draw through slip knot lp. Insert hook one mesh away, hook yarn and draw a lp through slip knot lp to make one chain stitch. Cont to make chain stitches through the mesh, working over every 1 or 2 mesh. Work in any direction, changing to 1 strand each of B and C held tog as desired until entire bag is covered.

KNITTED CORDS

Fringe loops

With 1 strand each of C and D held tog, spool-knit a cord that measures approx 90"/228.5cm. Fasten off, leaving a long tail. Thread tail in tapestry needle and weave through sts. Pull tail tight to gather, fasten off securely leaving a long tail for sewing.

Appliqué cord

Work as for fringe lps until cord measures approx 260"/660.5cm, using up rem ball of C.

FINISHING

Handle edging

With RS facing and working through both layers of mesh, sc handle edges tog along one edge using A, then along opposite edge using B.

Fringe loops

Sew each end of fringe lp cord to bottom side edges of bag. Form and pin 15 lps evenly spaced across bottom of bag, ranging in length from 1"/2.5cm at sides to a single 6"/15cm-long lp at center. Sew tops of lps securely in place.

Appliqué cord

Beg at front of bag, sew one end of appliqué cord to base of right half of handle. Measure 6"/15cm from end of sewn cord and mark with a pin. Sew cord to base of left half of handle at pin mark, forming a swag to hang bead doll. Cont to pin and sew cord in a freeform design over the surface of the bag, making sure to attach cord along center of both sides of each handle.

Bead doll

Select beads for head, neck, arms, hands, chest, hips, legs, and feet. Cut four 18"/46cm lengths of wire. Holding pieces together, fold in half and over cord lp at front of bag. Thread head and neck beads onto all 8 wires. Thread on right arm and hand beads onto 2 wires, bend back wires to keep beads in place. Thread on left arm and hand onto 2 wires; bend back wires. Thread on chest and hips onto 4 remaining wires. Thread on right leg and foot onto 2 wires. Bend back wires over foot, then tightly wrap 3 times around "ankle". Trim off excess wire close to work, then squeeze the wires with needle nose pliers to embed ends. Rep for left leg and foot. For each arm, bend back wires over hand, then tightly wrap 3 times around "wrist." Trim and squeeze wires as for legs and feet.

Beading fringe loops

Select one large bead and one small bead for each fringe, using the largest of the beads for the longest fringe lps. Cut eight 12"/30.5cm lengths of D. Split the yarn in half and use 2 strands for sewing. For each fringe, thread needle with one end of yarn. Insert needle into small bead; remove needle. Thread needle with both ends of yarn. Insert needle into large bead, then sew securely to bottom of lp.

NOTES

RESOURCES

US RESOURCES

Write to the yarn companies listed below for purchasing and mail-order information.

BERROCO
P.O. Box 367
14 Elmdale Rd
Uxbridge, MA 01569
www.berroco.com

CARON INTERNATIONAL
P.O. Box 222
Washington, NC 27889
www.caron.com

CLASSIC ELITE YARNS
122 Western Avenue
Lowell, MA 01851
www.classiceliteyarns.com

COATS & CLARK
Two Lake Pointe Plaza
4135 South Stream Blvd.
Charlotte, NC 28217
www.coatsandclark.com

FILATURA DI CROSA
Distributed by
Tahki Stacy Charles, Inc.

JCA
35 Scales Lane
Townsend, MA 01469
www.jcacrafts.com

KARABELLA YARNS
1201 Broadway
New York, NY 10001
www.karabellayarns.com

LANA GROSSA
Distributed by
Unicorn Books & Crafts

LION BRAND YARN CO.
34 West 15th Street
New York, NY 10011
www.lionbrand.com

LORNA'S LACES
4229 North Honore Street
Chicago, IL 60613
www.lornaslaces.net

MANOS DEL URGUAY
Distributed by
The Design Source

NASHUA HANDKNITS
Distributed by
Westminster Fibers, Inc.

NEEDFUL YARNS, INC.
60 Industrial Parkway PMB #233
Cheektowaga, NY 14227
www.needfulyarnsinc.com

PLYMOUTH YARN COMPANY
P.O. Box 28
Bristol, PA 19007
www.plymouthyarn.com

REYNOLDS
Distributed by JCA

ROWAN YARNS
Distributed by
Westminster Fibers, Inc.
www.knitrowan.com

TAHKI•STACY CHARLES, INC.
70-30 80th Street
Building #36
Ridgewood, NY 11385
www.tahkistacycharles.com

TRENDSETTER YARNS
16745 Saticoy Street
Suite 104
Van Nuys, CA 91406
www.trendsetter.com

THE DESIGN SOURCE
38 Montvale Ave
Suite #145
Stoneham, MA 02180

UNICORN BOOKS & CRAFTS
1338 Ross Street
Petaluma, CA 94954
www.unicornbooks.com

WESTMINISTER FIBERS, INC.
4 Townsend West
Unit 8
Nashua, NH 03063
www.westministerfibers.com

CANADIAN RESOURCES

Write to US resources for mail-order availability of yarns not listed.

KOIGU WOOL DESIGNS
RR# 1 Williamsford
Ontario, Canada N0H 2V0
www.koigu.com

NEEDFUL YARNS, INC.
4476 Chesswood Drive
Unit 10-11
Toronto, Ontario
Canada M3J 2B9
www.needfulyarns.com

PATONS YARNS
320 Livingstone Avenue
South
Listowel, ON
Canada N4W 3H3
www.patonsyarnsinc.com

S.R. KERTZER, LTD.
50 Trowers Road
Woodbridge, ON
Canada L4L 7K6
www.kertzer.com

UK RESOURCES

Not all yarns used in this book are available in the UK. For yarns not available, make a comparable substitute or contact the US manufacturer for purchasing and mail-order information.

ROWAN
Green Lane Mill
Holmfirth
HD9 2DX England
www.knitrowan.com

VOGUE KNITTING CROCHETED BAGS

Editorial Director
TRISHA MALCOLM

Art Director
CHI LING MOY

Executive Editor
CARLA S. SCOTT

Book Division Manager
ERICA SMITH

Graphic Designer
SHEENA PAUL

Instructions Editor
PAT HARSTE

Yarn Editor
TANIS GRAY

Technical Illustrations
ULI MONCH

Production Manager
DAVID JOINNIDES

Photography
JACK DEUTSCH STUDIOS

President, Sixth&Spring Books
ART JOINNIDES